A Paddler's Journey

Adventures on the water
and wisdom gained
along the way

Bryant Burkhardt

Bryant Burkhardt
Kayaking

ISBN-13: 978-0692471029 (Bryant Burkhardt)

ISBN-10: 0692471022

Cover & Back Cover Photos: Bryant Burkhardt
Interior Photos: Bryant Burkhardt, Krisztina Peterfy, Lindsay Burkhardt, Peter Burkhardt

To all the people who've shared the water with me: those who taught me when I was a beginner and those who still teach me as my students. To my friends and casual acquaintances, my readers and my role models. And to the best paddling partner I've ever found: my wife Lindsay – our journey is filled with far greater wonders than the physical world can produce.

CONTENTS

Foreword

My kayak flipped and darkness swallowed me. I reached my paddle to the surface to roll but hit something solid. I pulled my sprayskirt and kicked free of the kayak, the current shoving me against the back of an underwater cave. Rock surrounded me as I groped for a way out, or at least a pocket of air. Nothing. Lungs burning, I worked through my options. Several mistakes led me there: overconfidence in my abilities; underestimating the water; bad timing on my roll attempt. Knowledge, experience, and a little luck got me out.

How I arrived in that cave is the story of my paddling career. To understand how I stayed calm, you have to know my history. To appreciate my thoughts and emotions, you have to know who I am as a person. This book is about life lessons taught by the water, wisdom gained alongside paddling skills. My progression through kayaking and life. We'll get back to the cave, but we have to start at the beginning.

Bryant Burkhardt, June 2015

The author guiding a raft on vacation

Chapter 1

The Joy of Paddling

My earliest recollections of paddling involve sitting on the floor of an aluminum canoe in Minnesota, the metal cool against my legs as the summer sun bleached my pale blond hair. My dad steered from the stern and my brother manned the bow as we crossed quiet lakes to fish or floated down mellow rivers for the fun of it. I was as likely to jump from the gunwale and swim to shore as our golden retriever, Thor. The boat and the experience tied together in memory, a child's idealism connecting the two, I still feel the ease of summer every time I paddle a boat.

When I grew older, I received a paddle of my own and a plastic cooler to sit on. I struggled to match my brother's rhythm while my dad patiently let us sort things out. As the baby of the family and used to getting my way, it wasn't long before I usurped my brother's position in the bow. I wanted to be out front, the first one to reach any destination.

Together the Burkhardt boys were quite the formidable team. We glided across the water and paddled all day without rest, never getting wet—unless we stopped to swim. I'm sure my dad deserves the credit for our accomplishments, but I always felt like the captain since I sat in front.

One of my favorite trips was the annual church paddle, a social float, with a big picnic at the end. I considered it a race. Seven or eight years old at the time, I remembered the previous year when we were one of the first canoes to finish. This year, I wanted to be *the* first. I wanted to win.

The day of the trip I woke early, much to the surprise of my brother in the bottom bunk. My normal summer schedule involved sleeping in until the day grew warm and the community pool opened for sunbathing. But not that day. I wanted to make sure we got to the river ahead of the others. Start first, finish first—irrefutable logic to a child. I jumped down, nearly stepping on his head, and rushed to the dresser. He assured me that no one would start without us. Besides, we had to wait for our dad to pick us up. I pulled on some clothes, ate a quick bowl of cereal, and waited by the curb.

I squirmed in the back of the station wagon, straining to see the water as we dropped off our boat at the start and shuttled other vehicles to the take-out. River logistics didn't make sense to me. Why did we have to do so much driving? Why couldn't the car just be there when we finished? That was for the adults to figure out.

Everyone gathered for the safety talk at the put-in. Another thing for adults. I already knew how to canoe. I was a Burkhardt. So what if the river had some rapids on it, they were the funnest part. Of course I always wore my life vest, everyone knows that. Let's get on the water already.

But not everyone did know that. In fact, it was the first time canoeing for a lot of people. Even more had never been on a river. They paddled flat water and were understandably nervous about the current. And there were lots of kids. Someone needed to sort out who sat where in which boat, make sure kids had their life vests securely fastened, and carry the plastic rental canoes to the water.

My dad did those things because he could. He wasn't there to race. He had skills and experience which he used to help others; being strong and capable, he stepped in to do the heavy lifting. My brother assisted, most likely because it was the right thing to do. I did what I could, but only to hurry things along so we could get on the water. The incompetence of these people frustrated me as we cast them off, watching them slide down the river with an unfair head start. We launched dead last, me pouting, dry in the bow as my dad got his sneakers wet pushing us away. We would never win.

On the water I was the captain again. No more pussyfooting around—we got to paddling. I set the stroke rate and called when to switch sides. One, two, three, switch; one, two, three, switch. We moved that hunk of metal like a precision machine, gracefully avoiding slack currents and slower neighbors. We flew down the river.

In the distorted memory of childhood, I see a giant flotilla of canoes stretching endlessly down the grand waterway. An honest reckoning would be more like twenty canoes scattered along several miles of a peaceful stream. Whatever the count, we passed many and found ourselves near the front of the pack. The odd thing is, by that time I no longer worried about winning. The joy of paddling had taken over.

The splash of the water, the rhythm of the strokes, the cool breeze bringing scents of milkweed and wild sage, all combined to soothe my spirit and erase any thoughts of competition. It wasn't merely the happiness of being out on the water with friends and family but also a delight in the proficiency, the sense of knowing how to do something and doing it well. Making a connection with the water and using its power instead of fighting it. My family worked as a team in a way the other boaters did not. We possessed something special and had earned it through our experience. I didn't have the maturity to understand and express such thoughts, but they existed within me. That's what made me happy.

At the top of the biggest rapid, my dad pulled us into an eddy to wait for the trailing boats. I didn't complain. The race was over—we had already won. It wasn't about coming in first but about being paddlers, and paddlers watch out for each other. We sat there and enjoyed the moment. I waved to the kids going past while my dad gave advice to the adults. Hot dogs and potato salad waited downstream, but they could wait.

When the last stragglers approached the rapid, we started down with them. It was a shallow, rocky affair, with swift current that pushed boats toward the outside of the bend. As any good waterman knows, you need to keep the nose pointed downstream and stay to the deepest water. Even such a simple plan was beyond the capabilities of these greenhorns, and in short order one of the other canoes broached sideways, bouncing unevenly over the river's bed and doomed to be pinned on the rocks ahead.

My dad called forward paddle and I dug in with all the strength my slight frame possessed. Water flew from my blade as we rocketed forward, quickly catching up to the renegade vessel. My brother reached from his seat to grab their bow. I turned to watch with a mixture of understanding and awe as my dad leaned all his weight onto his paddle to keep us straight, wooden shaft flexing under the strain, and our momentum swung the other boat into line. Side by side we floated until I sliced my blade in and let the water pull us gently apart. With room to navigate, we both avoided the rocks and made it safely to the bottom of the rapid.

Instead of savoring our heroics, my dad steered us toward an empty canoe floating down the river with a father and daughter swimming nearby. They must have flipped with no one around to save them. Once again, we charged in with deft strokes to reach the pair quickly. My brother heaved the girl into our boat while my dad and I maneuvered. The man in the water hung on to our stern as we chased down their wayward craft and bulldozed it to shore. I leapt to the grassy bank and grabbed the bow while the swimmer caught his breath. My dad smiled at me and I glowed with pride.

Time spent draining the boat and sorting out its passengers allowed everyone to pass us by. We started last and finished last. No one else noticed; nor did they say who came in first, or even talk as if a race took place. Yet I still felt like a winner as I ran around the park, slurping sodas and devouring watermelon. To this day I feel compelled to help everyone get ready before we launch. I lift the boats for those who might have difficulty on their own. I work out the shuttle logistics, just so we get on the water a little faster. I learned more than the joy of paddling from my dad that day. Much more.

Chapter 2

THE PACIFIC

A s I grew up, I canoed less and less and became more interested in competitive sports: basketball, baseball, tennis. Like many teenagers, hanging out with my friends seemed more important that spending time with my dad. The occasional ski trip or a week of backpacking in Colorado, where he moved when I started college, brought us together, but the canoe was nowhere in sight. I spent a summer biking in the Rockies as I drove out to California to start graduate school at UCLA but never touched a blade to the water.

In Los Angeles the outdoors seemed far away. After two years at UCLA, I left with a master's degree in physics but stayed in the area for work. My roommate, Aaron, was still in the Ph.D. program, and I often joined him and the guys in his lab for adventures. RV trips up the coast of California, houseboat rentals on Lake Mead, or a weekend of camping in the desert. Stuff in the outdoors, but the days entailed little effort and ended with drinking beer and telling stories around a campfire. Adventure in a light sense of the word.

But one of the undergrads in the lab, Pedro, pushed for something more. He grew up in Cuba before immigrating to the suburbs of L.A., an easy smile on his face whether building an electron gun or grinding his mountain bike up a steep hill. He knew real adventure.

One of his favorite hobbies was sea kayaking, paddling the local coastline and nearby islands, most often by himself. He tried to share his passion with the rest of us. We always passed. Waves crashing on the shore, the sand littered with tourists and water-quality warnings. No thanks.

But Pedro suggested we go to Catalina, an island off the southern California coast, where the water is clean and crowds nonexistent, he assured us. A kayak rental shop sits where the ferry lands, and you can paddle right to the beach of a campground. The rangers will even truck your camping gear over so you don't have to worry about getting it wet on the trip. Nothing to it, he promised. No more excuses, we planned a weekend of kayaking and camping.

A short ferry ride from the metropolis brings visitors to an island with no cars and lots of open space. Most head to the city of Avalon, where nice hotels and fancy seafood restaurants await, but we took the longer ride to Two Harbors, where a small campground and single burger shack mark the jumping off point to explore the wilderness.

Our rental boats waited for us as we disembarked—all according to plan. The first indication Pedro's idea of easy differed from ours was that the ferry stops on the north side of the island, but the campground sits on the south. A skilled paddler can make the trip around the west end of the island in half a day. We had no skills and no intention of paddling that far. Luckily, the island is rather narrow—the landing area is called Two Harbors because it practically straddles both sides, each containing a well-protected cove. Pedro said we could carry our kayaks from one side to the other. No problem.

Carrying kayaks isn't hard if you double up: one person in front, one in back, carrying a pair of boats between you. It's nicely balanced and works well to move the kayaks, say, across the parking lot or down the beach. Walking a quarter mile over a gravel road is a different matter. Especially with our wide, heavy, sit-on-top rental kayaks. The hike bruised thighs, strained fingers, and covered us in sweat from the summer heat.

Pedro didn't carry a rental kayak with the rest of us—he brought his own sit-inside sea kayak, complete with a cart to easily roll it along. He stopped repeatedly to let us catch up.

"That's it guys," he said. "You're almost there."

His encouragement was met with resentment. Steve, a grad student more accustomed to snack runs to the fridge than hikes across an island, expressed a sentiment shared by most of the group: this wasn't the easy jaunt we expected from Pedro's descriptions. It came out more like, 'You sonofabitch, Pedro'. It was the first time we cursed him and his superior equipment, but it wouldn't be the last.

At the water's edge we dropped our loads and collapsed in exhaustion. Exposed arms and legs turned crimson to match our flushed faces. Pedro promised the hard part was over, right at home in his element. Our glares did nothing to diminish his zeal. It's hard to stay mad at someone who's so damn positive all the time.

We recovered from the death march and eyed the clear water. Everyone was anxious to take a dip, but first we had to sit through Pedro's safety talk. Being an adult, I felt compelled to listen this time. He talked about staying together and following his lead, about the swells we'd encounter when we left the sheltered cove, about climbing back on the kayak in case it flipped over. He would make the decision to hug the shoreline or cut across the bay to the campground once he saw the conditions on the open sea. Everyone agreed with the same enthusiasm reserved for clicking an agreement to the terms of service on a website. We just wanted to cool off.

We got our wish when we hit the water. The Pacific Ocean is nowhere near the giant bath tub many people imagine. The water is refreshing, if not downright cold; summer temperatures peaking in the mid-sixties. On the sit-on-top kayaks, not only were we exposed to any water that splashed over the side, but the boats have scupper holes to allow water to drain out the bottom. The holes also let the ocean trickle up from below, leaving us sitting in a pool of water that quickly went from cool relief to shrinking the family jewels. But not Pedro. His sit-inside kayak separated him from the water, and his sprayskirt, a piece of nylon around his waist stretched over the cockpit to seal water out, kept him warm and dry. You sonofabitch, Pedro.

With our wet bottoms, we trailed Pedro through moored sailboats and out toward open water. Another difference in equipment became immediately clear: his touring kayak was much more efficient than our boats. We could barely go straight, much less keep up with his effortless paddling. Like a kindergarten teacher taking his class on a field trip, he stopped every few strokes while we bumped into each other and flailed our paddles. He tried to give advice, but we were too busy cursing his superior skills to listen.

I focused on figuring out how to use a paddle with two blades instead of one. That's really the difference between kayaking and canoeing, and it's a lot more significant than it might appear. The body mechanics are completely different: the muscles used, how you hold the darn things, everything is different. With a kayak paddle you naturally stroke on alternating sides, and don't have to switch your hands around like with a canoe paddle. In theory, it's easier to go straight and more comfortable to do while sitting down (vs. kneeling in a canoe). In practice, it was strange and awkward and consumed all my attention.

It surprised me when I looked up and noticed our simple plan had gone to hell in fifteen minutes. We weren't together and Pedro wasn't in the lead. He paddled frantically between everyone, trying to get the faster newbies to slow up for those having trouble. All spread out and each headed in slightly different directions, it was chaos. That's when we hit the swells—or rather, they hit us.

As a child, I spent some time in small power boats on the Great Lakes and experienced significant storm waves—overhead, crashing waves that send a little boat careening wildly. But ocean swell is something different. The sheer volume of water staggers the imagination, rising and falling on a grander scale, like a slow motion roller coaster. Sitting at the bottom of a trough, a hill of water perched above me, I feared the inevitable crash. But nothing happened. The wave would simply slide underneath, and I'd magically be at the top of the hill looking down at the ocean stretched before me.

Bobbing like corks, my companions appeared and disappeared from view. From the top I spotted whoever was out front and headed toward them. I hoped they knew where they were going. Then I would drop down and be alone for a moment, nothing for company but my sense of awe.

I would have been happy to continue like this for the whole trip, unconcerned about reaching any specific destination, but Pedro appeared at my side to update me, easily navigating the large seas. Boris, a Russian grad student and one of the guys out front, was seasick and wasn't slowing down for anyone. Giovanni, an Italian exchange student, went with him. That left me, Steve, and Aaron in the back. Pedro needed to chase down the frontrunners and guide them to the camp site.

"Stay together," Pedro told me, his words crisp. "Don't lose sight of anyone. Keep paddling."

He waited for me to nod that I understood. This wasn't happy-go-lucky Pedro, but a man concerned with a serious situation. It knocked me from my contented place. We were onto plan B, and he was counting on me. I nodded, ready to help.

Pedro pointed out a peak on the ridge ahead, a target that always stayed in view whether we were up or down on the roller coaster of water. "Head that way," he said before speeding away. I watched with jealousy as he effortlessly sliced through the waves. I wanted to paddle like that.

Instead, I slogged along with my companions, both out of their depth in the waves. Steve weaved across the ocean like a drunk driver while Aaron went straight and fast for ten yards, then spun out and had to reset. I knew enough about handling a boat to go in a straight line, but it took all my attention. Whether because of focus or fear, we paddled in silence.

Lost once more in my head, I didn't notice I had pulled away from my slower companions until a strangled yelp grabbed my attention. I turned in time to see Steve precariously balanced on his steeply angled kayak, holding the high end like he could pull himself back to level. He couldn't, and with a squeal turned into a gurgle, he flipped.

He popped up sputtering next to his overturned boat, grasping at the smooth bottom like a penguin trying to climb out on an ice sheet. The wind had increased and waves slid across the kayak and dunked Steve despite the flotation of his life jacket.

"I'm okay," he claimed when Aaron and I approached. "But I lost my paddle."

Aaron went after the paddle as I struggled to recall what Pedro had said about getting back into our kayaks. Something about climbing on and kicking your feet. Maybe I should have paid more attention to that safety talk.

Steve didn't seem to remember any more details, and every time he pulled himself up the bright orange boat flipped over on top of him. It spun in the water with Steve no closer to getting on top and quickly losing energy. He floated with his arms hooked over the side of the boat, too tired to speak, but I knew what he wanted to say. You sonofabitch, Pedro.

With no real plan, I pulled alongside and held his boat steady. He gathered himself for one more try, and I leaned across to pull on his life jacket.

"Kick your feet," I said. It must be important since Pedro said it.

With a grunt and a heave, he came out of the water surprisingly fast and landed across both our boats. Together our two kayaks offered a stable platform, and Steve took his time sorting out his seat and getting situated. Aaron brought the recovered paddle over and Steve said he was fine, even if his wide eyes and shaking hands didn't agree. Best to keep moving.

This time I stayed vigilant and close to the others. Steve went in once more, but both of us remained calm and repeated the earlier procedure. Piece of cake this time. Knowing he could easily get back in with some help, and concluding the water was brisk but not so bad, Steve relaxed a bit. That was all it took for him to stay on the boat and even paddle in a straight line. Amazing how often our fear of an outcome actually manufactures it.

The three of us found our rhythm and enjoyed the rest of the paddle. Not far from the beach, Pedro showed up to guide us in, his easy smile back in place with the others already safely ashore. We scanned the water ahead and noticed the offshore rocks and breaking waves between us and our sandy destination, a minefield of white explosions and potential disasters. Thankful for the guidance, we followed Pedro on a circuitous route to within spitting distance of shore.

Before Pedro could give any advice about landing a kayak through the surf, Steve and Aaron headed in—they wanted off the roller coaster. Steve got tossed from his boat one last time before he could make land but simply stood in the shallow water and walked his boat the rest of the way. When a small wave picked up Aaron, he jumped off his boat and let the wave push his kayak to shore. Pedro rewarded my patience by telling me the secret: follow behind the wave, don't get in front of it. I did exactly that and beached my kayak gently on the sand, barely getting my feet wet as I exited.

Seasick Boris had fully recovered once on solid ground and shared his vodka with everyone. Steve warmed up in the afternoon sunshine, turning an ever brighter shade of red. Someone broke out chocolate from a pack, and we celebrated our survival sitting on the beach, looking out over the vast Pacific, the horizon a meeting of light blue and dark. Whitecaps glistened in the sun, and the breeze carried the taste of salt to our lips. Little waves lapped at the shore while rollers slammed into the rocks further out, sending spray high into the air. The combination of adventure and relaxation, excitement and contentment, remoteness and accessibility—that's what kayaking meant to me at that moment and what drew me to the sport. I wanted more and it didn't take long to get it.

The day was still young and Pedro eager to take his kayak back out for a little surfing. I had no idea you could surf a kayak. It wasn't something you did in Minnesota, and I had the vaguest notion of how it worked. No one else was interested, but I quickly donned my life jacket and snatched my paddle.

The waves on the beach were too small to ride, so Pedro took me farther out, to one of the reef breaks. Here the bigger sets broke as they passed over submerged rocks, the white foam spilling forward into deep water and safety—the perfect learning environment.

At first I watched Pedro position himself just behind the reef, pointed toward shore and looking over his shoulder. When a big wave came—all of four feet high—he slashed quickly with his paddle to accelerate and get in front of the reef where the wave picked up his stern, shooting him forward. He'd ride it out, gliding in his sleek kayak until the wave died, then circle back to set up again. It wasn't the North Shore of Hawaii, it wasn't even the small beach break of Santa Monica, but the energy of the wave gave him a ride and that's surfing.

My turn. I lined up like he had, watching over my shoulder. A wave came, not really big but big enough for me, and I paddled as hard as I could. The wave bulged up slightly and rolled under me, leaving me behind it, paddling uphill. Maybe I needed a bigger wave.

I lined up again. When the big one came I repeated my attempt. This wave did break, ever so slightly. It quickly turned my kayak sideways and nearly knocked me from my seat. I dropped my paddle and clung to the boat until the wave released me. Pedro caught the next one and smiled as he effortlessly flew past. You sonofabitch, Pedro.

The third time wasn't the charm. I didn't even manage to keep my seat as the wave broke on top of me, spinning me around and over. The cold water wasn't a shock at this point, but a salty nose-full made me snort. Having learned a thing or two from watching Steve, I kicked my legs behind me and threw myself across my boat. I landed on my belly and twisted into my seat on the wide kayak. It was kind of easy once you figured it out.

I spent the next half hour trying to catch a wave, any wave. Pedro raced passed me time and again, yelling encouragement. Maybe it was my equipment, maybe it was my lack of skill, but I never caught a ride that day. It didn't matter. Once again, there was no race, no competition. Being out there was the victory.

As the sun dipped toward the horizon, Pedro and I headed back in to help the others pitch camp. We spent the evening around a fire, roasting our dinner on sticks, reliving stories from the day. The curses for Pedro grew more colorful and good-natured. As the sun set, the sky matched the orange flames and more vodka warmed our spirits and swelled our imaginations. The waves in our recollections had already grown to giant tsunamis, flinging us about the angry sea. We had been bold and fearless and conquered the mighty ocean. And tomorrow waited for us to do it all again.

I stayed outside after everyone else had turned in. Stars spilled across the cloudless sky, a far richer tapestry than the city provided, combining with the gentle slap of the waves to lull me into a drug-like stupor. As I lay on my back, I still felt the up and down of the water, the sway of the ocean a part of me now. That sense of being on the water after you return to land is an after-effect of fluid sloshing in the semicircular canals of your ear. But it's also something more, not at all connected to the physical body. A feeling I wanted to keep.

The next day we returned the way we came. The waves were smaller but the wind was stronger. Pedro didn't bother with a complex plan to keep us together. We started with plan B: Boris and Giovanni sprinted ahead to avoid seasickness; Steve, Aaron, and I stayed together; Pedro paddled between the groups to make sure everyone was all right. This time we started with a high landmark on shore we could aim for. It worked all too well and the trip was uneventful. I still enjoyed it, but part of me missed the adventure, the sense of wilderness the ocean provided. I was addicted and needed a fix. You sonofabitch, Pedro.

Peaks rising straight out of the water

Chapter 3

NORTH TO ALASKA

Life often gets in the way of living. I returned from Catalina eager for more kayaking but worked six or seven days a week. I taught test preparation classes for college entrance exams in the evenings and on weekends. My only outdoor pursuit entailed the occasional walk to the office on a sunny day, dodging traffic and breathing smog. After a couple years, I longed for adventure—any adventure. I looked north to Alaska.

Be it biking in the Rockies or climbing in the Sierra, the mountains always delivered great times and memorable experiences. Alaska operated on a bigger scale and promised more of the same. I set my eyes on Denali National Park with visions of tromping over the tundra dodging brown bears and moose. Escape into the wild. A daydream that kept me entertained while sitting at my desk.

Winter approached—not the time to head north—so I squirreled away my vacation days and planted a flag on the calendar for the following summer. Alaska or bust. My roommate Aaron had time between research projects and vowed to join me—Catalina had whetted his appetite for adventure as well. We invited Pedro, but his schedule (and fiancée) didn't allow for it. He had already sketched out a couple of dream trips to Alaska and shared his ideas. One involved climbing Mt. Denali—too cold and technical for us.

Another was sea kayaking in Prince William Sound. That sounded interesting.

Southeast Alaska is a kayaker's dream, the waters surrounded by tall peaks and glaciers tripping into the sea. The Sound itself consists of many bays and inlets protected by outer islands that deflect Aleutian storms. Rugged and beautiful; sheltered and safe. Outfitters offer guided trips with no experience necessary, catering and boat support included. Not quite the adventure I wanted.

A little more research led me to a place that rents kayaks for self-exploration. Based out of Whittier, it was the perfect launching point for a multi-day trip. They also arranged for a water taxi to drop us far from civilization. It required adding an extra week to the vacation plan and the skills to do it safely.

The extra time turned out to be no problem. I quit my job the day after Christmas. I had no plan for my future, no sense of what I wanted to do with my life. Might as well spend some time exploring the world and doing things I enjoyed.

The skill acquisition took more effort. First, I asked Pedro to teach me how to use a real kayak like his. No more plastic sit-on-tops; we were going to use sit-inside sea kayaks and needed to learn the basics. Pedro applauded my desire to learn but turned me down flat. He knew how to kayak but not how to teach kayaking. It's a wise man who knows the distinction.

He pointed me to UCLA's recreation department. I had learned rock-climbing through them and participated in several trips with their Outdoor Adventures program, but I never noticed their off-campus facility in Marina del Rey that taught sea kayaking. They even offered a discount to alumni, perfect for a man without a job.

My formal education began in the descriptively named Sea Kayaking 1 on an early spring weekend. Four fellow students braved the gloomy marine layer and constant sailboat traffic to learn basic strokes and rescues. Our instructor was an undergrad from Santa Barbara who sounded like he'd rather be out surfing but put up with us and our silly questions in a good-natured manner. We wore black wetsuits and orange paddle jackets, covered by bulky yellow life vests and blue vinyl spray skirts. All fashion sense left in our wake, we gathered on the dock to learn how to wet exit.

Getting out of a sea kayak is an easy thing to do when it's sitting on shore. When it's upside down, you're underwater, sprayskirt holding you in the boat, the process can be scary and seem difficult. To overcome this claustrophobic experience, most programs teach a simple step-by-step procedure to follow when the boat flips. Standard protocol is to have each student demonstrate/practice a wet exit in a controlled environment before doing anything else on the water. We took turns using a boat tied to the dock as surfer-boy gave us encouragement.

When my turn came I wasn't nervous; I'd flipped a kayak before, in surf no less. The shock of the cold water changed everything. This wasn't Catalina in the sun. The water was ten degrees colder, and the jolt of immersion was followed by the seep of chilly seawater into every nook and cranny of my wetsuit. It also flooded my nasal cavities and overloaded my mammalian brain. My reptilian reflexes took over and after thrashing free of the boat and gasping for air when I hit the surface, I swam frantically away from my boat and over to the dock. With a complete lack of grace, I hauled myself out and lay shivering.

Not exactly the controlled procedure we were going for. My only condolence was watching the others do the same. Saltwater slowly leaked from my nose as the next in line repeated my performance. Kayaking wasn't as fun as I remembered.

Paddling around the marina and practicing stroke technique warmed me. It wasn't scenic or adventurous, but it felt good to learn how to steer. We played around and figured out what worked and what didn't, the instructor giving some pointers as he passed by. Compared to a sit-on-top, the boat was fast and efficient, responding to my actions like it believed I knew what I was doing. This was more like it.

Then it was time to get back in the water to learn rescues. No problem, I had done this before as well.

Once again, things were different. The cold water hadn't gotten any warmer and numb fingers made everything harder.

Narrow sea kayaks aren't as stable as wide sit-on-tops. When I tried to throw myself across it like I had the sit-on-top, the boat flipped. I had to straddle it like a horse—a technique called a cowboy scramble. Sitting on the deck raises you high above the water and makes the whole thing as tippy as a bowling ball on ice. It took a couple tries before I got back in; most of the students never succeeded. The process filled the boat with water, making it wobbly to the point I could barely paddle. Why is a sit-inside a better design again?

Surfer-boy earned his pay and showed us another way to re-enter the boats with assistance. Kind of like the way I had held Steve's boat so he could climb aboard, but with specific changes for the sit- inside kayak. First, he lifted the bow of the upside down boat and drained the water out. Then he held the kayak steady as the swimmer climbed onto the back deck.

"This is the counter-intuitive part," he said, directing the person to lie on their stomach facing backward on the boat. He helped them slide their feet into the cockpit and they spun around to face forward, ready to paddle. We partnered up and tried it ourselves, everyone able to get back into their boat this time. It wasn't that hard when you got the hang of it, but it required two people who knew what they were doing and how to work together.

The day was full and I learned a lot. I felt good about my successes and had a newfound appreciation for the sport. But it had all been inside the marina, on flat water near shore. We hadn't ventured out into the swells, much less tried to handle the surf. I needed a lot more training and practice to be ready for Alaska.

Onto Sea Kayaking 2. This time the instructor and his assistant were both PhD candidates—professional, fun, and most importantly, they knew kayaking. They put everything in a broader context: the stroke is short because that's where it's efficient, the blade goes out from the boat because that's where body kinematics work best. Sit-inside kayaks have many advantages, including stability in rough water and greater control over the boat. With their ability to demonstrate and the knowledge to explain, the instructors' quick review of Sea Kayaking 1 taught me more than the entire previous day had.

We moved on to new environments and topics and went out past the breakwall to practice rescues in the confused chop near the rocks. Same technique, different medium. All the little points became important, like tucking the paddles into your stomach to keep them from drifting away and leaning across both boats to stay stable in rough seas. My confidence rose to another level. Not only could I do the rescues, but I would be able to do them when needed.

We talked about navigation, using transit points on shore to register drift from wind or current. They taught us strategies for dealing with fog, using the angle of the swell for direction and the sound of breaking waves for guidance. We landed and launched through small surf on Venice Beach. Their instruction was the same Pedro gave me back on Catalina— follow the wave in, don't ride it—but I couldn't resist the chance to use my faster boat to catch a wave, paddling hard to get in front and feeling the rush as it propelled me toward the sand. The moment of joy was worth the wipeout that followed, and my silly grin got a laugh out of the teachers when I dragged my boat ashore.

Beyond simple fun and basic skills, our instructors offered us something more valuable that day: a passion for kayaking (and the results it brings). They paddled with proficiency and precision, laughing and enjoying their day with us because they were on the water, and any day on the water is a good day. They inspired us.

After class, I talked with them about my plan for Alaska. Neither had been there, but they were full of little tips that proved helpful later on. Things like getting multiple small dry bags so they pack into a kayak easier and studying the tidal exchange in the area so you don't get stranded by an ebbing tide. They also suggested I learn to roll.

One of the major advantages of a sit-inside kayak is that if you flip over you can roll back up without doing a wet exit. It's the safest and quickest rescue, and absolutely essential in many situations. Rolling isn't that hard to do, just rather hard to learn. Something about trying to remember a sequence of body movements while upside down underwater boggles the human mind. The answer is learning through repetition and muscle memory, which takes time and persistence, and a good teacher.

Next class: Kayak Rolling. Taught in the pool over two days, I was the only one in the class who succeeded on day one. But I only did a single roll, and every other attempt ended in failure. It took another couple of hours on day two to get the correct motion wired in for a consistent roll. Success gave me a feeling of satisfaction, a sense of pride reminiscent of my joy of paddling a canoe as a child. Doing something was never enough—I had to do it well.

I now considered myself a kayaker though an inexperienced one. In the time remaining before our trip, I sought out as much experience as I could, renting kayaks from UCLA to practice my rescues and work on my endurance. I convinced Aaron to come out for a session so we could work on rescues together, going from student to teacher and foreshadowing my future in the sport. He had no desire to learn kayaking for its own sake; he simply wanted to use a boat to get to someplace special, but he mastered the basics, and I knew he'd handle himself well in an emergency. I was the kayaker, in charge of that portion of our trip, and its success or failure rested on my shoulders. I judged us ready and off we went.

Aaron and I arrived in Alaska the last week of May, well into California's summer but Alaska still waited for spring. When we got off the train in Whittier, a fresh dusting of snow covered the six-foot-high drifts which buried the sidewalk, and a cold fog lay like a wet blanket over everything. The town was still asleep, so we wandered the empty streets, gravity pulling us down to the harbor. The water was as featureless as the sky, a void of pale light and unknown intentions. Dipping a hand in confirmed it—we were far from Catalina.

When the town began to wake up, we met the outfitter at the docks. Bob was a native Alaskan, with long hair, rumpled clothes, and a broad smile. He tossed his cigarette and shook our hands with a bone-crushing grip, offering coffee black, apologies for no milk or sugar. We discussed the weather as strangers often do, but with more urgency on our part. Was the snow going to affect our plans? Any storms in the forecast?

Bob shook his head and leaned against the deck rail, assuring us that this *was* summer in Alaska, often taking the full season to melt off the winter's snow. Nothing to be concerned about and no problem for the kayaks. His appraising glances suggested he didn't have the same faith in us. He pushed himself up and sauntered over the boats laid out before us.

The white and yellow kayaks were long and high volume, made of fiberglass and decked out with rudders and compasses. Far more beautiful than the cheap plastic boats at UCLA. It was both exciting and daunting to use such expensive and high-performance equipment. Bob walked us through the adjustments for the foot-pegs and how to raise and lower the rudders. He gave us a patch kit in case of an accident but assured us we wouldn't need it. Again, fully confident in his equipment.

Bob and I confirmed the details we'd gone over on the phone. The water taxi would take us out and come back to pick us up three days later. We'd stay inside the one bay, where the ocean was flat and tour boats passed frequently. Bob provided a marine radio that worked over line-of-sight. We could contact any boat by hailing it on Channel 16, but only if we could see it; the radio would never reach all the way back to Whittier. We'd be the only kayakers out there, and no one could hike in through the snow. We'd have the place to ourselves for the most part, but knowing that people would come through occasionally and be able to help in an emergency was reassuring.

Bob checked out our camping gear and approved—it was good backpacking equipment, small and light. The only thing that didn't pass inspection was our footwear. Bob didn't want the glass kayaks getting scratched when landing, so he gave us knee high rubber boots to get out in shallow water and walk them carefully to shore.

"What happens if you capsize in the boots?" I asked.

"They sink," Bob said. "So don't capsize."

Good advice.

He also pointed out that the water was one degree above freezing. In water that cold, you have less than a minute before your body loses all manual dexterity and a rescue becomes impossible. His additional advice: if you do capsize, be damn quick about getting back in the boat. Hard to argue with his logic.

Soon a boat arrived and Bob helped us load the water taxi. It wasn't even nine a.m. when we motored out of the harbor and headed up the coast. A dense cloud cover hung a few hundred feet off the water, hiding the surrounding mountains and making for a dull ride. It took an hour to get to the beach at the mouth of the Barry Arm, entrance to the Harriman Fiord and our home for the next three days. We unloaded the boats and did a quick check of gear before our taxi driver headed back for his next fare. The sound of his engine slowly faded into the distance as we packed up the boats, easily fitting our small dry bags into the watertight hatches.

Once ready to launch, we stood a moment, taking in the solitude. The clouds had risen slightly, affording us a hint of the peaks that must lie above, and a mist floated in the air, covering everything with a layer of moisture. The call of distant birds echoed across the still water. This is what we came for, but doubt crept into my mind. Are we ready for this? It's the question that begins every great trip, and the answer is only found one way. We slid the kayaks in the water and started out.

Unwilling to disturb the music of nature, we didn't say much the first hour, the rhythmic splash of our paddles the only sound of our passage. Hugging the shore, we could see the deep snow piles between the Sitka spruce and western hemlock. Small chunks of ice floated past, calved off the glaciers beyond our sight. Lost in thought, enjoying the beauty, a splash behind my kayak broke the spell.

I twisted my neck and caught a glimpse of something large and brown diving under the water, then nothing. We were within a boat length of shore, a rocky cliff about ten feet high. Aaron took off at a sprint.

"Was that a bear?" he asked. "I think that was a bear."

Instinct and intellect fought. Part of me wanted to join Aaron in his mad flight from danger. This was bear country and bears can swim. But it was black bear country. And bears, particularly black bears, don't chase down kayaks. I paddled after Aaron while watching over my shoulder, my strokes calm and measured while my pulse raced. Seconds added to fill a minute, all calm on the water. A bear couldn't hold his breath for that long. Right?

Another loud splash made me jump (well, as much as one can jump while sitting in a kayak). This time I saw the cause: a massive brown head broke the surface with a sharp exhalation of air. I smiled and let out the breath I hadn't realized I'd been holding.

"It's a sea lion," I called out to Aaron, who was far ahead and still cranking. "I think it's one of those Steller sea lions. They're big." Indeed, this one was twice the size of the California sea lions I normally encountered on the rocks in Marina del Rey. As big as a bear. But while they might bark fiercely, they're generally harmless. This one was spy-hopping—bursting out of the water to look around before slipping back under. A prime example of the nature we came to see, and I poured on the speed to catch up to Aaron. The adventure had begun.

We took a break for lunch on a sandy beach, hopping out in the calm water with our rubber boots to save the kayaks any wear and tear. I pulled out cans of tuna from our lunch bag, and we headed to the tree line to eat. Prepared to give Aaron a hard time for being afraid of bears, I choked back my words when large tracks dotted the sand. At the trees we found bear scat, smelling all too fresh. We walked back to eat near the boats with our eyes scanning the shadows under the trees. The unknown puts you on edge, and it wasn't until we paddled away that conversation resumed.

By then the mist had turned to a light rain and what little scenery we had disappeared into the gray. Our rain gear kept us dry and our thermals kept us warm, but the flatness of the day soaked into our spirits. While our nerves settled down with the repetition of strokes, it wasn't the exuberant experience I hoped for. We called it an early day when we found a nice beach free from bear signs. We set up camp, cooked dinner, and read in the tent. A perfectly fine and safe start to the trip, but I went to sleep hoping for more.

The next day dawned with the same flatness, and at three in the morning. Summers that far north are blessed with more daylight than your body knows what to do with. After waking up to a slow, pale sunrise, it took hours of restless tossing before I ignored the light and returned to sleep. Eventually Aaron and I both straggled out of the tent halfway through the morning. A slow start with our biggest day of paddling ahead did not bode well, but the long days also created a large margin for error. Everything would work out.

This was our day to see glaciers. That's what the tour boats came for, and why we picked this location. Three glaciers came together at the top of the Barry Arm and slid ever-so-slowly into the ocean. If only the weather would cooperate and give us some views before we ran straight into them.

We paddled along shore and I noticed the things I had missed the day before. Cormorants drying their wings like old men in ill-fitting suits, oystercatchers with bright red beaks squeaking as we passed, colorful sea stars clinging to the rocks as the tide ebbed. Up in the trees, bald eagles sat patiently, waiting for a school of fish to get pushed to the surface by an underwater predator before swooping down to grab an unlucky herring. Nature surrounded us and made us welcome, we only had to open our ears and eyes to take it in.

It wasn't far to the first glacier, and the ceiling of clouds lifted as we rounded a point to reveal its majesty. A towering wall of white ice loomed over the water, jagged cracks slicing its face. It climbed up a steep mountain valley and disappeared white into white. Over the ridge to the left was its bigger brother, another glacier at the water's edge, with a third sibling less than a mile away. Without a word, we stopped paddling and floated in awe. This was why we picked Alaska, why Aaron bothered with the kayaking, and I took all those classes. It was more than worth it.

We landed at a nearby rocky shore, flat enough to climb out and pull our kayaks secure above the water. We hiked to the glacier, our rubber boots crunching on the snow. The clouds dissipated and the sun came out, sparkling off the white powder and dazzling us with glimpses of dark blue ice buried beneath. We returned to our kayaks for lunch, no thoughts of bears to distract us from the beauty of the place. All was right with the world. Then we heard the first explosion.

A loud crack was followed by a giant section of the middle glacier collapsing into the water. The splash shot high into the air and waves radiated out. A mile away, it felt immediate and close. More chunks fell into the water, most the size of a car but some as big as a house, or even an entire apartment building. Nature put on quite a display. We took in the show, and all the ice that fell into the water drifted slowly toward us. In fact, the entire bay was filling up with icebergs. Very pretty, but our destination lay across the bay. Time to get moving while there was still open water to paddle on.

"Will it cut us off?" Aaron asked, stuffing the lunch sack back into his boat, spurred to action but the uncertainty of the situation.

"No, we'll be fine," I assured him.

"What if it hits the boats?"

"They can handle it."

But I secretly shared his fears. I wouldn't have been so worried in a plastic kayak, but the ice looked solid and sharp, and fiberglass boats were new to me. Maybe a jagged edge could crack them, flooding them with water and sending us to a frozen grave. We both paddled a little faster as we crossed.

All my kayak training paid off as we dodged through the ice flow, using sweep strokes and bow draws to nimbly maneuver between chunks. Aaron copied my lead though not as smooth or precise in his strokes. As my fear of getting trapped faded, I became more conscious of my enjoyment.

Knowing how to paddle, doing it with some skill and style, planning a trip and executing it, felt very natural and proper. I was fulfilling my purpose.

We reached our desired campsite without incident and settled in for the evening. The glaciers still calved and ice steadily floated past, and the sky eventually cleared, revealing the breath-taking view of Mt. Gannet rising ten thousand feet straight out of the water. It would have been nice to enjoy a sunset, but that wouldn't happen until after midnight and the next day was our last—we needed to get to the pick-up spot early. As pleasant as the trip had been, getting stuck out here for an extra day wasn't an option. We had even more adventures awaiting us on land.

Acclimating to the daylight, we managed a good night's rest and rose at a reasonable time to get under way quickly. Our concerns melted away, no longer worried about ice or bears, comfortable in the boats and our ability to cross the bay, able to enjoy the tranquility of nature around us. We reached the beach with hours to spare before the water taxi was scheduled to arrive, and I used the time to dream of my next trip, my next chance to kayak. I still had two weeks of backpacking and fishing across this bold state, but my mind was connected to the water.

It wasn't just that we had avoided getting eaten – though that was nice. It wasn't just that I enjoyed the paddling. It wasn't the success, but that the success had been earned. I had prepared for the trip, put in the time to learn and practice skills, picked our destination and route, made sure my partner was capable of holding up his end. I was responsible for my own happiness, and happy I was. Back home I was a jobless, uncertain twenty-something with no plan for his life. Out here I was a kayaker, in charge of my fate and rewarded for my efforts. I held onto that forward momentum as long as I could.

Chapter 4

INTO THE SURF

I returned from Alaska and talked my old company into creating a new position for me. A job that would allow me to take a leadership role, help develop operational systems, and train others up and down the west coast. I would be based out of L.A. and have plenty of time to continue kayaking. Good life here I come.

But the company's VP had a different vision, and within two months he gutted my resources and twisted my role to suit his needs. I became a traveling troubleshooter, his hatchet man, sent from one crisis to the next. First Houston, then Seattle, Berkeley, San Jose, and more. Places with kayaking potential, but my days off infrequent and my energy level depleted. Most importantly, I had no control over my world and no creative aspect to my duties. Stressed out, overworked, living out of hotels, something had to give.

Spring found me in Santa Cruz, a laid back surfer's town with beautiful scenery and perfect waves. Time to grab a piece of life. I scheduled a rental at the local kayak shop, parking at a meter near the pier with a three-hour limit—a sad reminder that my time for fun was strictly limited. The boat waited for me on a floating dock, the only sea kayak among standard sit-on-top rentals. Much shorter boats lined the dock as well, sit-inside kayaks half as long as the sea kayak, with flat bottoms and hard edges. Excited to get back on the water, I didn't give them much thought.

The kid running the place handed me a paddle and lifejacket. When I asked about a sprayskirt, he said they didn't rent them out. Too dangerous.

But I had braved the wilds of Alaska, I explained. I knew how to do a wet exit, had practiced rescues 'til they were second nature, and could even roll the darn thing!

Didn't matter, policy was policy.

Disappointed, I took what I was given and expertly climbed into the boat from the dock, determined to show my skill in whatever way possible. My best forward stroke carried me swiftly away and down the coast.

I headed east along the boardwalk, feeling sorry for the poor folk stuck on land, riding a rickety old roller coaster as if it were exciting. The ocean was a much better ride, even if it was a small one that day, providing a freedom you couldn't get from a metal rail. I rounded a point and left the amusement park behind.

My life jacket fit poorly, the seat back rubbed my skin raw, and the paddle was short and heavy. I was happier than I had been in months. The water reflected the clear blue sky, only darker and full of mystery. Seagulls and pelicans flew overhead while seals and sea lions played in the rocks. A slight breeze stirred the air and kept me from overheating. It felt like home.

Like that, a decision was made. This is what I should be doing with my life. My own happiness and well-being were more important than the concerns of a corporation out to make profits. What that would look like, how I would make a living, I had no idea. But it would involve kayaking, of that much I was certain.

By the time I returned to the dock, five minutes before my parking meter was set to expire, countless questions swirled in my brain: what kind of jobs involve kayaking? Could I teach or lead trips? Could I do it based out of L.A.? I needed to learn more about kayaking as an industry and not just a sport. After checking in my boat and equipment, I took the time to ask about the little sit-inside kayaks. With a nod toward the other side of the pier, the kid said they were for surfing.

Over there lay Steamer Lane, one of the most famous surf breaks in the world. My mind raced at the thought. I knew you could surf a sea kayak, but what would it be like in a small and nimble craft? How do you get enough speed to catch a wave? How hard are they to roll? How do your legs fit inside the little things? Time to start answering questions instead of always asking them.

First, I notified my company that I was no longer going to work on the road. My gig in Santa Cruz was up in two weeks and afterward I was headed home. If they could find a role for me in Los Angeles, I'd be happy to do it. If not, so be it. They made no promises and I expected none.

Next, I checked the rental company for surf kayak classes. One was scheduled for my last day of work. The universe approved my plan. A quick email informed my apathetic boss I was quitting a day sooner than expected. I didn't get a reply.

The surf class was small, only four students. The instructor was a Santa Cruz local who board surfed as well as kayak surfed. He fit us into plastic whitewater kayaks, rough and plain next to his sleek and shiny composite boat. He assured us that we'd appreciate the forgiveness of our boats, that his surf kayak was much harder to roll. And rolling would be a big part of the day.

We didn't go to Steamer Lane but the much smaller break inside, where little waves gently washed up on a sandy beach. The first half hour of class was talk and flat-water paddling. The instructor described the timing, how you had to start paddling before the wave reached you and stop once the wave took over. We worked on our acceleration, quick forward strokes to catch the wave before it passed, and stern rudders, the way to steer once in motion. He asked if people wanted to practice their rolls before hitting the surf. It was a chilly morning and the water was downright cold—we all passed. I hadn't rolled a kayak in almost a year, but I assumed it was easy to remember, like riding a bike.

The first wave went right under me. Short boats are much slower than long ones, and I totally mistimed my effort. I caught the next wave and experienced a moment of exhilaration before the nose of my boat buried itself at the bottom and I pitch-poled over like a dolphin flipping in the air, only with none of the grace, style, or gentle landing. I slammed head first into the water and continued to get spun like a load of laundry as the wave carried me with it. White bubbles surrounded me and sunlight circled wildly, destroying my sense of up or down. The water tried to rip the paddle from my desperate grasp, but I hung on, knowing it represented my only chance to roll up. I tucked into my set up position and waited for a moment of calm. When the wave released me, I started my roll.

Apparently rolling a kayak in the surf is not like riding a bike. It's more like riding a unicycle on ice with your eyes closed while getting pelted with snowballs. That's how it felt as I floundered, yanking on my paddle, straining my neck to barely break the surface and snatch a quick breath before setting up to try again. The next wave came and took me for another wild ride, leaving me more confused than before. This time I gave up, pulled my sprayskirt, and swam out of my boat. I breached the surface like a spy-hopping sea lion and sucked in the oxygen needed to get my brain working again.

The instructor had told us what to do in the event of a swim—he was realistic about our chances of rolling in the surf. I held onto my paddle and got on the ocean side of my kayak so a wave wouldn't slam it into me. I pushed it forward and swam toward shore, letting the waves take the boat to the sand as I followed behind. When I could stand, I grabbed the handle at the font of the kayak and pulled. It didn't budge. Water weighs eight pounds a gallon and my little whitewater kayak held sixty gallons of water or more. That's several hundred pounds. I tossed my paddle above the water's reach and tipped the kayak over. The effort left me sitting on my butt, sucking air as the water drained out the cockpit.

The whole time I smiled. Maybe not while under water, but as soon as I came up I'm sure I had a smile on my face.

Even when the cold infiltrated my wetsuit. Even while I struggled with the heavy boat on the sand. Especially as I watched my classmates wiping out and copying my swim to shore. I had surfed a wave for half a second and it felt great.

I repeated the process for the rest of the class. My rides got longer, my wipeouts less violent, but most waves ended with me upside down and completely unable to roll. The instructor offered some tips on rolling, but I chose to spend my time surfing instead of practicing in flat water like he suggested. I got very good at swimming and emptying the boat, timing my launch from the beach, and swimming in waves. I took a beating but it was worth it.

Riding a wave felt like I had tapped into the very soul of the ocean. I accelerated down the face, a rush of speed and possibility, the weight of thousands of gallons of water pushing me forward. The power of the water coursed through the boat and every inch of my body. When the wave broke, walls of foam collapsing in a thunderous roar that engulfed my insignificant craft, I disappeared into a different realm. The water swallowed me, absorbed me into its fold and took me along as it spilled its energy, eventually dying in a sublime trickle of little white bubbles on the sand. The transformation to my psyche was immediate and my future clear.

The next day, as I made my way down to Los Angeles, I stopped at a kayak shop to pick up a wetsuit of my own, along with a paddling jacket and personal flotation device (PFD— that's what real kayakers call a life jacket). Their new kayaks were rather expensive for the recently unemployed, so I decided to look for a used one, searching the classifieds before I unpacked my car.

An internet ad led me to an outfitter in San Diego selling off its whitewater fleet. I knew nothing about what makes a good surf boat, but the guy told me the little orange one was perfect. It fit me tight and looked similar to what I had used in class, with a rounded front and flat tail. I paid cash and he threw in a sprayskirt and paddle. I was ready to surf. Well, except for that rolling bit. I needed to work on that.

I turned to the only kayak expert I knew: Pedro. More than willing to help me with my roll, he shared his good news about surf kayaking. While I traveled for work, he had bought himself a whitewater kayak and went surfing once a week with another paddling friend. Pedro also had a pool at his apartment complex which he frequently used to practice his roll. Apparently regular practice is essential if you want to keep the skill. Useful to know. It only took half an hour with his guidance to get my roll back. The next day we headed to Topanga for a surf session.

Topanga is next to Malibu, a small public beach snuck in between million dollar homes. It's a point break, waves spilling cleanly off a bit of land sticking out into the ocean. It's one of the best surf spots on the most crowded, surf-crazed coasts in the world. Not only is it popular, it's 'owned' by locals who are very territorial. Board surfers often dislike other board surfers who invade their space. They hate kayakers.

In their defense, kayaks can be dangerous in the surf. They can't get off a wave as easily, making it harder to avoid collisions. Our boats are not tethered to us, and a fourteen-foot sit-on-top without its rider is a steam-rolling log that can wipe out an entire lineup. Unskilled kayakers are dangerous. Skilled kayakers can be worse—they have more maneuverability and can chase down waves easier and catch them further out. Nobody likes someone who steals their fun.

The easiest way to avoid these problems is to avoid board surfers. That's what we did. In addition to the crowded main break at Topanga, there's a secondary break. It's not as big or as easy to catch, so it doesn't attract the boardies, but it's perfect for a kayak. We caught ride after ride and Pedro taught me about surf etiquette, the other way to avoid problems with fellow wave riders. Take turns, give priority to those in the best position, stay in control. Not all that hard.

Topanga became a weekly session. Pedro and I would meet up with Elliot, an area local who kayak surfed well enough to earn the respect of the boardies. We stayed off the main point and stayed out of conflict, occasionally getting a shout of profanity from the lineup or dirty look on the beach.

But Elliot was as laid back as Pedro was good-natured, and I followed their lead and had nothing but positive vibes for our fellow wave riders. Through routine and repetition our skills increased and our presence was tolerated. We surfed other places—San Onofre, Manhattan Beach—but Topanga was our local spot.

I improved quickly as a kayaker. Nothing like a pummeling to motivate you. My roll became bomb-proof on both sides. I learned to rudder with my paddle and how to turn by edging the kayak. Side-surfing waves, dodging breakers, reading the swell, all became second nature. I was a surf kayaker.

As fall turned to winter, the days grew short and the swells grew tall. The surf forecast called for big waves arriving overnight and perfect conditions for the next day's dawn patrol. But Pedro and I couldn't wait and met the afternoon before at an empty beach. The waves small, the weather drizzly, no wonder no one was out there.

We geared up and went out anyway. Even without waves, kayaking is fun. For the first time, there were no board surfers at the point, none at all. Pedro and I made our own lineup and waited for the occasional two-footer to give us a short but sweet ride. In between sets we talked about life, about other kayak adventures we would have one day, about nothing at all. Each set grew a little larger and they came more frequently. Soon we rode three- and four-foot waves, the tide filling in and lengthening the rides. Surfers appeared in the parking lot.

They weren't the biggest, but they were the cleanest waves we ever had, and Pedro and I rode them with style. We hit bottom turns and cutbacks, threw some floaters off the lip, and deftly carved around the surfers swimming out to join the lineup. Maybe it was because we had been there first, maybe it was because we showed some skill and control, but no one questioned our presence. We greeted the newcomers with big smiles and waited our turn. People asked about the changing conditions and we reported what we'd seen. Everyone caught great rides.

By the time the light started to fade, two dozen boardies bobbed around us at the point. The waves were five to six feet and forming perfectly, but the wait for your turn was long. Pedro and I wished everyone well and headed into the beach. We didn't pack up and leave, but stood onshore in our wet gear and watched the sun set behind the surfers, sky turning from blue to orange to gray. They were our brothers out there; we belonged as part of this community, even if our craft was different. We had earned our spot. The smile on my face was the same one I found in Santa Cruz, the one that started in Alaska, or maybe Catalina. The Pacific was my home now.

Chapter 5

Those Who Can, Teach

All I wanted to do was kayak, but I needed to eat and that meant work. Temporary jobs, like intranet design or curriculum writing, which allowed a flexible schedule and plenty of time to surf. I made enough to survive and fuel my kayaking habit, but there was no future in it. I didn't know what my future held, only that it had to include kayaking. So, how to make my vocation into an occupation?

Having taught all my life, from tutoring friends in high school, to working as a teaching assistant at UCLA, to training test prep instructors for my old company, teaching kayaking seemed the obvious choice. I could make a living doing that, right?

I started with the only place I knew that offered kayak instruction: UCLA's Marina Aquatic Center (MAC). The instructors for my courses there had even suggested I become an instructor, but at the time I was gainfully employed and more interested in playing in boats than working around them. I called them up to offer my services and find out what such a job would entail. It was the middle of winter, so kayak classes were done for the season (yes, in spite of the mild weather there is a non-kayaking season in Los Angeles. What can I say, Southern California makes you soft.). But as luck would have it, their instructor training course was right around the corner.

The training course made me a little nervous. I was very comfortable teaching things I knew well, but how much did I actually know about kayaking? Was I really any good at it? It's very hard to judge yourself, especially with only a small reference group. Sure, I had survived Alaska, but we had very mellow conditions the entire trip. Surfing was fun, but it was very different from paddling a sea kayak. My roll was reliable, but I hadn't practiced other rescues in a long time. I looked forward to meeting more kayakers and improving my skills, but part of me worried about living up to my own expectations. Pride is a delicate thing.

Not a single familiar face greeted me at the MAC the first day of training. None of my previous instructors were there; I didn't know any of the other instructor candidates. The first thing they told us was the man who had started the program and been its leader for the past decade was leaving. A team of replacements would be our trainers and this was their first time. Not the most reassuring start.

Then we got into the training. Introductions revealed most of the candidates had as little experience as me. In fact, my surfing time and ability to roll garnered several looks of admiration. We talked about learning and teaching styles, new terms but familiar concepts for me. We hit the water to practice strokes, and in addition to getting technique pointers myself, I watched the others and decided I was on par skill-wise. When we divided up to do rescues, the techniques came back to me and all went well. I settled in and relaxed. I was going to be fine.

The training involved five separate sessions, including one at the pool and one in the surf. At the pool, it surprised me to learn that only a couple other candidates could roll their kayaks. What I considered a necessity to be learned early in one's paddling career was regarded by many sea kayakers as an advanced skill that wasn't needed for most people. In the surf, waves that disappointed me in their small size intimidated many in the group. Again, lots of paddlers stick to flat water and leave the surf for experts. I didn't consider myself an expert, but clearly my experience and learning curve had not been typical.

The whole course was enlightening, not to mention fun, challenging, educational, and rewarding. The other trainees became friends and paddling partners. The trainers did a great job—the program in good hands with its new leadership. At the end they invited me join the ranks of MAC instructors. A part-time job, but the first step on a new journey for me.

They also suggested I consider getting certified as an instructor. I had no idea what they were talking about.

The American Canoe Association (ACA) is a non-profit organization dedicated to educating the public on water safety. In spite of the canoe in the name, they also deal with kayaking, rafting, and stand-up paddling. Their goal is to keep people safe when playing on the water, whatever form it takes. Along with public outreach, they also offer certifications for instructors. The training program at the MAC was modeled after ACA guidelines, and a couple of the leaders were already certified. If I wanted to be a professional kayak instructor, ACA certification was the way to go.

While it was great that a national organization offered official recognition of skills, and encouraging that these guys thought I was worthy, it also meant another opportunity for my lack of experience to be revealed. For all my success as a paddler, I didn't yet believe in my skills. I felt like I was in a small pond, and as soon as I got out into the big ocean of kayakers my deficiencies would show. My goal of becoming a kayak instructor was already fulfilled. Did I really need to test myself again?

The answer was yes—I always needed a test. I wouldn't be satisfied until I had proven, mostly to myself, that I was good enough and worthy. That pride thing again.

I enlisted help right away. I worked with one of the MAC instructors who was already certified. We went over paddling technique, we talked about tides and navigation, and he warned me about the rigors of the certification process. Those doing the certifications, called Instructor Trainers, were demanding, and the standard was a high one. Intimidated and motivated, I signed up for the first ACA course on the calendar.

There's a two-step process to become an ACA certified instructor. The first step is a three-day development workshop. The Instructor Trainers running the course show you all the skills you need in order to get certified. You also get the chance to demonstrate what you can do and receive feedback on your technique and teaching style. There's no pass or fail, it's just about participation and learning, so there shouldn't be any pressure. That's saved for the second part, a three-day certification exam where you are evaluated and judged on everything from demonstrating strokes to handling group management scenarios in rough conditions.

The only certification courses in the state took place in the San Francisco Bay area, well known for its fast currents and cold water, things unfamiliar to me. I showed up at the development workshop with the same old doubts. Am I any good? At this level? How will I compare to these paddlers?

This time introductions didn't erase my worries; I was clearly the least experienced of the group. The other candidates included a professional guide from Alaska (I didn't even mention my little trip for fear of sounding like a tourist), a couple local instructors who had taught for years, and one gentleman who'd been paddling for two decades. Most had their own boats and equipment, including some composite boats nicer than anything I'd seen. I had borrowed a plastic sea kayak from the MAC, along with most of my gear, and felt like the little kid trying to fit in with the big boys.

My concern only lasted until we got in the boats. On the water, the playing field leveled out. My technique was as sharp as anyone's, and I knew the current teaching methods since the MAC's program was nearly identical. Years in the classroom made me comfortable in front of an audience and gave me experience most kayakers don't have. When we had a playful race before lunch, I reached the beach before anyone else. From that point on, I knew I could hang with the pros.

In the remaining two and half days I learned a lot, including that there was always more to learn and room for improvement. A new world of information opened before me and it confirmed my experience thus far had been sheltered.

But I could handle it. The positive feedback from the Instructor Trainers, both women with exceptional skills and tons of knowledge, helped my confidence, but the acceptance from the class as one of the guys proved more than anything that I belonged.

Unfortunately the next certification course that fit my schedule was six month away. I returned to the MAC and spent a summer teaching kayaking, surfing with Pedro on off days, and paddling every chance I got. My pride had been satiated in the courses, and I was free to enjoy the experience of teaching and continue to improve as a paddler. The more I let go of my concerns about being good enough, the better I became, both as a paddler and an instructor.

By the time certification came around, it seemed like an afterthought. In my mind, I already was a professional kayak instructor; I got paid to teach and I did it well. My students were happy and successful. I got the certification, passing the course with no worries, and continued on my career as a kayaker.

Kayak Polo at UCLA

Chapter 6

KAYAK POLO

At our monthly meeting, one of my fellow UCLA kayak instructors announced that a new sport had started on campus. A husband and wife from New Zealand, electrical engineers working at the UCLA Brain Institute, had formed a kayak polo club which met at the pool once a week. Games were open to anyone who wanted to learn how to play.

I had no idea what kayak polo was, but the name intrigued me. Growing up in a small Midwestern town, sports largely defined a person's identity. I judged myself and was judged by my success in baseball and basketball. I switched to tennis in high school and went on to play in college. Organized competition was part of my life long before kayaking, and combining the two sounded perfect. I turned up at the pool the next week with my whitewater kayak and gear, unsure what to expect but excited to give it a try.

A compact Saturn wagon piled high with several kayaks and lots of plastic piping strapped to the roof pulled into the unloading zone. A couple in their mid-thirties climbed out and introduced themselves as Paul and Katherine. Their Kiwi accents and cheerful manner immediately made me feel welcome.

Other members showed up to carry the equipment poolside. It took several trips to empty the car crammed with paddles, helmets, life jackets, blocks of foam, and rolls of duct tape. Everyone did their best to explain the game as we made several trips to get it all poolside.

"It's like water polo, but with kayaks."

"You pass the ball with your hands—but you can also use the paddle if you want."

"The goals are suspended above the water and you use a paddle to block shots."

"Do you know how to kayak?"

Yeah, I could kayak, so I figured I could handle this game. How hard could it be?

I joined Paul and Katherine at one end of the pool with a pile of PVC pipes. As they explained the rules in more detail, they expertly put together the piping, connecting pieces like a three-dimensional puzzle with the competence you'd expect from a pair of engineers. A plastic tower arose and a rectangular frame with netting stuck out, about the size of a hockey goal but six feet off the ground. I helped them slide it to the edge of the pool and it hung over the water, its twin put up at the opposite end by the other folks.

Next, they showed me how to tape a thin plastic strip around the edge of my paddle to prevent the blades from cutting people when fighting for the ball. More tape secured foam to the ends of the kayaks, padding the tips so the boats wouldn't stab a person when they collided. They also loaned me a helmet with a facemask of wire mesh. How dangerous was this sport?

Katherine must have noticed my apprehension because she laughed and assured me everything would be fine. Impossible not to trust her smiling face, I hopped in my boat and joined the others paddling around the pool to warm up. At least paddling was something I knew how to do—then someone threw me a ball.

I instinctively dropped my paddle and caught it. My kayak turned and its momentum carried it straight into the concrete edge. The foam bumper absorbed the impact and I tried to pass the ball back. I missed by ten feet.

Throwing a ball when you're sitting down is hard. Throwing it behind you because you can't turn around is harder. Doing it all while floating on the water with no support makes you feel like a clumsy kid. I doggy-paddled myself away from the wall, picked up my paddle, and rejoined the group. By watching the others, I figured out little tricks to the sport. Instead of dropping their paddles, they caught the ball with one hand and used the other to steer the boat. When they threw the ball, they twisted their torsos to leverage their body. By pushing the ball down its buoyancy popped it out of the water, much easier to grab. The concept of the sport may be simple, but the execution requires many skills.

After our warm-up, we divided into two teams for a friendly game. Katherine captained my squad and Paul the other.

"Do you know how to roll?" She asked.

I confidently replied yes.

"Can you roll without the paddle?"

I waited a moment to make sure she was serious and shook my head. She said we could work on that next time, then announced to everyone that since it was my first night, no one was allowed to push me over. Not sure if I should be offended or relieved, I charged in when a whistle started the game.

Too much happened too quickly and I felt like a dog chasing a Frisbee. I had no trouble with the kayaking, but I couldn't keep track of the ball, my paddle, my teammates, and the rules. You're not allowed to hit people with your paddle or boat, but I fouled everyone in spite of my best intentions. Every time I sprinted in one direction possession changed, and everyone was going the other way before I could react. More than once the ball hit me in the head because I was too busy watching the other players to see it coming. Paul and Katherine were experts, but most of the others had only been playing a few months, many with rudimentary kayaking skills. They still played better than me. Those few months made a world of difference.

At one point in the game, Katherine held the ball, arm cocked to throw as Paul slid next to her. Before she could release the ball, he reached out and shoved her over—perfectly legal under the rules. But as fast as she went over she came right back up, nothing in her hands but the ball. She passed it to another teammate and the game continued, but my mind stuck on what I'd seen.

As I've said, rolling is a tricky thing to learn. Most kayakers I knew, including a number of instructors, worked on the skill for months or even years to master it. The most difficult part is timing the motion of the paddle with the rest of the body to make sure you get the maximum support from your blade at exactly the right time. But here was proof the paddle wasn't needed at all. Katherine rolled faster than anyone I'd seen. The rest of her boat handling skills were just as impressive. Paul never rolled because he never needed to; when people tried to push him over, he simply leaned his body into it and kept his balance. The abilities on display in the pool far outmatched what I was capable of. It was humbling to be a novice again.

The next week and every week after, I returned to the pool for more education. Paul and Katherine were always ready to teach. The time and effort they put into teaching not just me, but everyone at the pool, was inspiring. They also designed and built the goals and loaned out extra equipment to anyone who needed it. They loaded all that stuff on and in their little car and toted it back and forth from their apartment once a week. Always with a smile. They taught me as much about the community of kayaking as the skills for kayak polo.

But teaching hard skills they did. Katherine taught me how to hand roll, Paul taught me how to control my kayak with body weight instead of a paddle. They showed me how to throw a ball with power and use my paddle to block a shot. My skills increased quickly and before long I played as well as the other newbies. Paul and Katherine were happy enough with our progress that they decided to host a tournament with clubs from San Diego and San Francisco. Time to learn teamwork.

A kayak polo team consists of five players on the pitch (the water equivalent of the field of play), with up to four others waiting to sub in. You're not allowed to paddle when you have possession of the ball, so passing and coordinating movements are key. In order to have a reasonable chance to score a goal, you need to get in close without many defenders in front of you, using screens from your teammates and fighting for position. One player can't accomplish much on their own. It's a team-oriented team sport, more similar to soccer than basketball. Paul and Katherine knew what they were doing, but the rest of us were clueless.

We did the best we could in our weekly practice sessions. We tried to set screens and work the ball around the perimeter, but we often lacked enough people for five a side, so we scrimmaged three on three in a pool shorter than regulation. Our still-developing skills made it hard to get any rhythm going, too many dropped passes or errant shots to really learn how things should work. We competed against ourselves, and that lack of competition gave us a false sense of achievement. We thought we were ready for the tournament. Ready to play, sure, but nowhere near ready to win.

Luckily our first game was against San Diego. Their club had formed a year earlier, and Paul and Katherine had helped them develop before founding the UCLA club, so they were a little more advanced than our group. But Paul and Katherine carried our team on their backs, and my paddling experience and sports background made me one of the stronger players to support them. The game was tight and I felt like I could stay close to the San Diego players, but not quite catch them. Their passes were crisper, they reacted faster, and they didn't make as many mistakes. We gave a spirited fight, I scored one of our goals, but we lost by two. A good match.

The game against San Francisco was an entirely different matter—they scored on us in the first ten seconds. After winning the sprint for the ball to start, they came at our defense en masse. I was out front, tasked to stop them from penetrating our line. Before I could put a blade in the water, one of them sprinted past me like a cheetah hunting a gazelle. As I turned to chase him, another guy paddled right over the top of my boat. The ball went over my head, one of them caught it and threw it into the net while our goalkeeper futilely waved his paddle. An inauspicious start.

They were the defending national champions, with several Europeans who grew up playing kayak polo, and they had played and practiced together for years. It was a whole team of Pauls and Katherines, only stronger and faster. The rest of the game was more of the same. I couldn't believe how fast they were in their polo-specific kayaks, carbon composite boats half the weight of my plastic one. They had low volume sterns that the players used to slice into the water and pivot a hundred and eighty degrees faster than I could turn my head. Their paddles were carbon as well, blurs of black that stopped my passes and shots. More importantly, they knew where everyone was and worked as a unit. Whether it was on defense when they shifted together to block an attack, or on offense where they always managed to find the teammate who had the best position to shoot, they played together and out-smarted us. Paul and Katherine had similar skills, but they were saddled with us rookies. We had to take time to figure out what to do, and even if we had the time we didn't always come up with the right answer. It wasn't a fair fight.

The final score was twelve to nothing, a huge discrepancy for a twenty-minute game. I had no pride at the end of the game, but I did have a resolution. I wanted to be that good one day; to play like the San Francisco team.

The challenge of learning new things got me interested in kayak polo, but the chance to be part of a team kept me there. Over the next months and years, I greatly improved my skills as a kayaker in general and polo player in particular. I continued to surf and paddle on the ocean, I even learned how to whitewater kayak. But I stuck with polo because I liked being part of a team, especially Paul and Katherine's team.

Chapter 7

WHITEWATER

Playing kayak polo made me feel more like an experienced kayaker. Maybe not an expert, but someone with skills and competency, and most importantly, I understood the principles. I got it. In my mind it was only a matter of time and practice before I reached the expert level. The same on the ocean; my path was clear and I headed down it with full confidence I would reach my goal. When I started on the river, the route was harder to find.

Paul and Katherine were avid whitewater kayakers, coming from a small island country with giant mountains and raging rivers. Kayak polo is a fun pastime in New Zealand, but whitewater kayaking is a national obsession. When the snow in the Sierra started to melt, they headed for the rivers and tried to drag a few of us polo players along.

I was interested but not driven. The closest river was the Kern, outside Bakersfield three hours away. Trips happened on weekends when I taught my sea kayak classes or went surfing with Pedro, only twenty minutes from my door. And I was already good at those things. It took until mid-summer for calendars to align and Paul and Katherine to organize an introductory weekend on the river.

We started in the pool, one of our evening polo sessions given over to practicing whitewater kayaking skills. We learned things we thought we already knew, like how to accelerate and turn our boats. Paul drilled us with a fervor and urgency well beyond our polo lessons, exhorting us to imagine current, water pushing against our boats. We did our best but apparently came up lacking.

"You have to edge more," he'd say.

I'm edging as much as I can, thank you very much.

"Your timing is off."

Off from what? Where's the imaginary current again?

The session frustrated me because I thought I did everything fine, but according to Paul none of us were getting it. Of course, he said it in a nice way and with a cheery expression, but it still hurt to fail. We didn't understand what it was. It turned out to be current, and the pool sorely lacked any simulation of it. Perhaps that's why only three of us beginners trekked up to the Kern that weekend.

The Kern River starts atop Mt. Whitney, the highest point in the contiguous United States. It crashes down through steep mountain valleys, different forks joining and swelling the flow until it's stopped by a man-made wall of concrete creating Lake Isabella. Then it's metered out carefully to run one last steep canyon filled with power generating turbines and finally diverted into irrigation canals. It limps out of the foothills into a dry desert and trickles down a few small rapids before it's swallowed up by the earth completely, not a drop making it past Bakersfield. We started at those last rapids, the grandeur of the river lost but its nature still intact. Current existed here, real and substantial.

Orange groves and ranchland lined the banks and we camped in a park with grass gone brown in the summer heat. Our first morning consisted of paddling in circles, in and out of the current. Now we understood how much we needed to edge our kayaks; timing our strokes with the water became obvious. The concepts were clear enough, my brain understood, but my body didn't cooperate. Yes, I had paddled rivers in a canoe as a child, but that experience was far removed. I kayaked now, in the ocean and the pool. My skills weren't developed with current in mind. I struggled.

To be fair, I did fine for a beginner whitewater kayaker. I flipped a few times, but I rolled up with no problem, navigating most rapids upright. By your average measure, it was a complete success. In my mind, it was a disaster.

On the river I was no longer an experienced kayaker. I wasn't in control. I lacked the smooth strokes that carried me so well on the ocean. As hard as I tried, as much as I listened to Paul's advice, I couldn't force myself to do things right. That first day was humbling and challenging. I can't even say if I enjoyed it—I was too focused on the minutia of what I was doing to look up and see the world around me and have any appreciation for it. An evening spent around the campfire with good friends relaxed my spirit, but my thoughts never settled in one place.

The next morning we headed up the canyon to a new section of river. We stopped along the road to watch water cascading over giant boulders, creating waterfalls twenty feet high. Yes, people kayak down that, Paul assured us with a hint of longing in his voice. It was so far beyond my ability to comprehend I merely shook my head and enjoyed the beauty.

We drove around Lake Isabella to Kernville, a quaint mountain town nestled in the southern end of the Sierra Nevada on the banks of the Kern. A grassy park, still green along the river's edge, made a perfect warm-up spot. A hundred yards of easy whitewater to paddle down and then walk back up for another lap. We set up shop for the morning and continued our education.

Once again, I struggled with the basic approach to river running. Paul and Katherine stayed positive and offered nothing but smiles and encouragement. But I was frustrated. The main idea on the river is to lean away from the current, letting the water pass underneath the boat. Otherwise the current can grab the boat's edge and flip it. On the ocean, you lean into the wave. Physically, it's for exactly the same reason—the wave pushes you over the water, creating an effective current, and you raise the far edge to let the water go underneath you. Mentally it's the difference between a positive (lean toward the wave) and a negative (lean away from the current). While my body waited for my brain to sort out the direction, the current did its work and over I went. Often.

Watching Paul and Katherine didn't help. They made it look all too easy. Never a bobble, never a rushed stroke, they didn't seem to be doing any complex calculations in their heads. They read the water and knew what to do without a second thought. I could mimic their movements, but without knowing when or why the results were quite different. After a morning of repeating the same short stretch of river over and over, I made it down without flipping but knew I hadn't mastered any general principles.

Lunch was a needed break and a chance to enjoy the surroundings. We were in the mountains, a new town but a familiar atmosphere. The air was thin and the afternoon wind rustled the leaves on the trees. The sun warmed us as we sat on the bank and dug into the cooler for cold drinks and homemade sandwiches. The idyllic setting did more to attract me to the sport than anything else. Kayaking under the mountains had been a highlight of the Alaska trip, and whitewater kayaking promised many such landscapes, if only I could master paddling in current.

After lunch we drove upstream to run a new section of river, rated class II on the difficulty scale (rivers are rated from class I—small splashes—up to class VI—unpaddle-able). It wasn't remote and wild, just a short stretch from a powerhouse down to town, passing houses and an RV park along the way. Still, going downriver provided more adventure that doing laps in a park, and I needed something new to judge my progress. This was our final test for the weekend, multiple rapids over several miles that ended in the biggest—a three-foot waterfall just upstream of the park. If we survived, we could call ourselves whitewater kayakers.

We put on the river and followed our fearless leaders into the unknown. Shallow water and lots of rocks filled the first long rapid; I bounced my way down keenly aware that Paul managed to avoid all the rocks I hit. But my boat was made of hearty plastic and I had enough skill to go in the same general direction without getting stuck. Small successes.

The powerhouse fell behind and greenery surrounded us for a stretch. In that calm part of the river, where I could float along peacefully, the sense of belonging returned to me. A boat that floats, a little cool water, some nature and good friends. That's all it took to make me happy. Then we stopped to scout the first big rapid of the run.

The drop was relatively short but steeper than anything we had done before. The route was straight down the middle, but the whole river abruptly turned left. Jagged rocks lined the shore and a concrete wall at the base of a riverside mansion hemmed in the water. The consequences of a mistake were clear—anyone upside down could get banged up pretty bad.

"Are you ready?" asked Paul.

Us three newbies shared a look of apprehension but still nodded yes.

"Right," he smiled at us. "Let's give it a go"

We followed the pattern of the weekend: Paul in front and Katherine at the back, the three beginners between them with me in the middle—I had the most reliable roll so I was farthest from help. It had worked up to this point.

The water leading into the rapid was calm, making it easy to start in a straight line. Paul hit the waves first and bounced up and down as relaxed as ever, pointing right down the middle. The person in front of me entered the rough water and veered wildly, heading toward the rocks. I came next and chose to follow Paul, relying on my experience in waves to steer straight and make the crucial left turn when it came. My wayward companion spun out and faced the wrong direction, stuck in a small eddy along the wall but still upright. Self-preservation far outweighed any sympathy and I paddled past, eyes glued to Paul's tail. I hit the bottom pool that marked the end of the rapid and flew into the eddy behind Paul, both of us turning to watch the rest of our party come down.

The person behind me came through fine. Katherine stopped to help the person who had gotten turned, and they both finished the bottom section cleanly. We all floated in the eddy with large grins. Maybe we did have some skills after all; maybe we could do this. We peeled out of the eddy and continued on our merry way.

A couple smaller rapids lay between us and the final challenge. My confidence restored, I handled them with ease. Everyone in the group felt good as we eddied out above the final rapid to go over the plan. It was too long to scout the entire thing, so we relied on Paul's memory and description to guide us. This one wasn't quite as simple. The route was to start right, cut over to the left, and then back to the middle to finish it off. We couldn't see it from our vantage point, but the final drop was the largest, a mini waterfall between boulders. After that it was all done, so no worries. I've since learned that when a Kiwi tells you not to worry, that's when you should start.

In my customary position in the middle, I kept my focus on Paul up ahead. The maneuvering wasn't hard, but it slowed us rookies down. The group spread out and I lost sight of Paul at the critical moment when he cut back to the middle above the final drop. I followed my fellow beginner and her performance didn't inspire confidence. She cut back toward the middle, but didn't make it far enough. She went off the left side of the three-foot waterfall and flipped on the landing. I charged hard right but had no idea where to aim. I went over the drop and a cross current hit my right side. As my brain registered this and worked on the math to sort out the correct reaction, and my body waited for the result, the river impatiently flipped me over.

I had been upside down plenty of times over the course of the weekend and many times before that in the surf. Sometimes you get spun around, and often it's hard to figure out which way is up, but the water normally moves you along, eventually releasing you into a calm spot. In a hole on the river, like the one I found myself in, the water recirculates. It doesn't go anywhere. I did what I had always done and rolled up, only to be in the same place with the river doing the same thing: it tossed me hard. This time my reactions were even slower, I didn't manage to tuck and protect myself. My paddle hit a rock with my arms extended and something in my shoulder popped. All thoughts of rolling disappeared. I immediately dropped my paddle, pulled my sprayskirt, and kicked out as hard as I could.

Paul was occupied helping the first swimmer to shore and yelled for me to grab my boat and swim it to him. I did the best I could with one arm. When I reached the shallows and could stand, Katherine came in with the third swimmer in our group hanging off the back of her boat. None of us beginners made it over the falls in our kayaks. I sat heavy on a rock and let the sun warm my body as pain spread through my shoulder. I wasn't sure about this whitewater kayaking.

The summer wore on and the river dropped down. Paul encouraged me to give whitewater another shot before the season ended. I hesitated. My shoulder had been sore for a couple weeks but had healed up fine, so that wasn't a good excuse. I just didn't know if I wanted to do something I wasn't very good at. He assured me that I did fine for my first time out; he had swum a lot more when he first started. I had all the skills needed and more time on the river is all it would take to develop them. His faith in me far exceeded my own, but I didn't like the idea of giving up. I decided to risk injury to body and pride for the chance at redemption. My teaching schedule was full, but I had one Sunday off in August and agreed to meet Paul up in Kernville.

This wasn't a beginner training trip. Paul was up paddling for the entire weekend with friends from San Diego, hitting the hard stuff on Saturday. I drove up that night to meet the group at a cabin in town. It was the hottest weekend of the summer, still over one hundred degrees when I arrived after sunset. A driveway full of kayak-laden cars marked the right house and voices from the deck above floated down as I approached. A deep baritone rose above the rest, recalling a particular rapid from the day and pointing out in great detail what went wrong and why. In the darkness I couldn't tell how many people were in the group, or even recognize Paul among them, but the speaker stood out, a large man of middle age, with a bushy mustache glowing white in the moonlight. Paul noticed me and interrupted the soliloquy to make introductions.

The owner of the mustache also owned the cabin. Gilbert welcomed me to his place warmly—if I was a friend of Paul's, I must be good people. A slew of other names passed by but didn't register, some familiar from the polo tournament but hard to recognize in the dark.

After the introductions Paul apologized but had to leave—a work emergency called him back to L.A. He assured me I was in good hands; Gilbert would look out for me. I found an empty camp chair and sat quietly, listening to the conclusion of the day's recap.

They had run a class IV stretch of the river, with a number of swims and some carnage, though nothing too serious. The group had a wide range of abilities, some very experienced and some as green as me. Everyone looked forward to an easier day tomorrow, and that sounded good to me, even though I wasn't exactly sure what constituted easier for them. If Paul said I could handle it, then it must be okay.

When the last stories had been told, everyone grabbed a sleeping pad from inside and claimed a piece of the deck. A spot in the corner served as home for the night, and I listened to the snores of my neighbors, sleep far away. I stared up at the stars thinking about the next day, nervous about how I'd handle the river, afraid to embarrass myself in front of a bunch of strangers. Deep thoughts and unanswered questions came and went long after I closed my eyes, but eventually I drifted off to sleep.

The next morning was a slow start followed by a lesson in efficiency. Everyone slept in until the sun rose high enough to crest the far hill and raise the temperature twenty degrees, propelling everyone into action. Gilbert ran the kitchen like a drill sergeant, handing out tasks and barking orders, swinging his spatula like a baton. I received patient instructions, but the regulars, those who should have known better but were slow to respond, received biting comments from the mustached commander. I fell in line and did what I was told, including eating more than enough pancakes to suffocate the butterflies in my stomach.

Plans were made to run the section of river below the lake, a new one for me. Shuttle logistics were taken care of by those knew what they were doing, and I went along for the ride. It was like my childhood canoe trips all over, only this time I knew enough to be afraid.

Gilbert took me under his wing for the trip, and the first thing he did was insist that I demonstrate my roll. Paul's recommendation and my assurance weren't enough—he needed to see it with his own eyes. Fair enough. In the calm water where we started I rolled several times—it was nice to cool off as the temperature already topped one hundred degrees. Gilbert critiqued my form but said it would do. I passed the test.

Once everyone was on the water and headed downriver, I noticed two things that were different from my previous river paddles. First, this wasn't a class. Gilbert gave me some guidance, knowing every rock in the river like the layout in his pantry, but I wasn't expected to blindly follow him. Everyone else was busy having fun and zipping around. It wasn't about learning anything particular or practicing skills, it was paddling for its own sake. People looked out for me but only in the way they looked out for each other, not the way an instructor hovers over a student. I could do what I wanted; if I screwed up, no big deal.

Second, the scenery was beautiful. The run started in a quiet campground with a mini-gorge of white granite walls, and while the road was nearby it was out of site. The river wound through a deep canyon, with riparian forest at the river's edge giving way to brown, grassy hillsides above. This was kayaking in the wilderness, and once I felt comfortable enough to look up from the whitewater, I enjoyed every minute of it. I was hooked.

Another thing that greatly eased my mind was the fact that I wasn't the only person flipping over. Even the most skilled members of the group were playing around, sliding up rocks and trying to get their kayaks vertical. In the process they frequently failed and flipped over. It was a part of the sport, nothing to be ashamed of. I played around too and flipped over more. Sometimes we rolled just because it was so damn hot. In the first big rapid I collided with one of the other guys, and we both flipped over and rolled up laughing. This was fun.

At the end of the day I still sucked as a whitewater boater. It felt unnatural and I often leaned the wrong way or reacted too slow. I lacked the skill to help in any significant way. I didn't even know the logistics of the run to help with shuttle. It didn't matter—it was still a good day. I didn't have to be perfect, or even good. I didn't have to impress anyone. All I had to do was keep trying and have fun. That's all they expected of me, that's all anyone wants on an adventure. I made the right choice to stick with it. Too bad the season was over.

Chapter 8

The Channel Islands

With the rivers dried up I turned my attention back to the ocean. Getting a taste of wilderness made me hungry for more. I wanted another adventure like Alaska, but without the expense of flying to a faraway land. Luckily, the unknown existed right in my back yard, and the invitation to go explore arrived at my doorstep.

It came in the form of a trip announcement on a local paddling email list. Joe, a kayaker I'd never met, planned to paddle the four northern Channel Islands and he invited anyone with the necessary skills to join him. The voyage involved long distance ocean crossings, possible rough water, and primitive camping out of kayaks. Over six days it would cover one hundred and twenty-five miles. Only experienced paddlers need apply. Sounded perfect.

I sent two emails, one to Joe to say I was interested, and one to Pedro to see if he was as well. Joe invited me to a test paddle and Pedro said hell yes. In addition to our surfing over the past year, Pedro and I undertook several sea kayak outings, including a trip back to Catalina, covering more ground and camping around the island before paddling back to the mainland. He always wanted to visit the rest of the Channel Islands and now I did too.

Pedro and I drove to the test paddle together, a day trip out and back to the closest island, Anacapa. Twenty-two miles round trip. Launch time was six in the morning and part of the test involved packing all your camping gear and being ready to go on time. It was dark when we arrived at the put-in, headlamps bobbing back and forth between the parking lot and the beach, a dozen kayakers rushing to get ready.

One of the guys strolled over and introduced himself without any urgency. Duane was his name, and he wasn't packing because he didn't need to pass the test, he was already on the trip—in fact, he helped Joe plan it. While he asked about our background in a friendly manner, Pedro and I unloaded our boats from the car. Our actions spoke louder than our words as we efficiently loaded our boats and geared up, ready for launch in no time. I immediately liked Duane for his critical eye and relaxed manner, and he seemed to appreciate our competency and cheerfulness in the early morning hour.

At exactly six a.m., Joe stood in front of the boats and addressed his troops like Patton on parade. He would lead the group and expected us to keep up with his pace. People could stop on the island's lone beach if they wanted, but those who hoped to join the expedition needed to stay in their boat the whole time—you can't hop out to stretch your legs on an ocean crossing. If there was time, we'd practice rescues at the end of the day. With that he dragged his long, carbon-kevlar boat into the water and paddled away. We all hustled to follow.

The pace was fast but nothing I couldn't handle, Pedro was a speedster and keeping up with him had trained me well. The sun lightened the sky and I took stock of the group. Fifteen paddlers in total, one lone woman among a group of old men—Pedro and I youngsters in the crowd. Everyone else paddled composite sea kayaks, sleeker and faster than our plastic boats. Decks lay buried under charts, compasses, GPS units, and other paraphernalia I didn't recognize. A lot of money was on display, and I assumed a lot of skill and experience went with it. I felt inadequate.

We stopped for a quick break at an oil rig a few miles off the coast. Joe reminded us that the shipping channel started soon and we needed to cross with all haste to avoid being run over by a tanker. They move five times faster than us, and it takes over a mile for them to stop—not that they would for kayakers. They'd probably never see our tiny boats and mow us down without noticing. I appreciated the excellent visibility that day and swiveled my head constantly to check both ways as we headed out.

I hung close to Joe, eager to learn a little more about the person in charge of the upcoming expedition. Duane stayed close as well, an old friend of Joe's but the polar opposite. Joe ran his own consulting firm, a self-made businessman who was proud of his success and ambition. Duane had been a long-haul truck driver and currently worked as a private investigator. Joe appreciated order and structure, and could tell you his average speed over the course of any paddle and what time we should reach shore to the minute. Duane shared stories of insurance scam artists he followed for his job and was more likely to match his pace to a pod of dolphins than worry about what time we'd make it back to the beach. On the water they complimented each other just fine.

No tankers appeared during our crossing and we reached the island in no time, spurred on by Joe's drive and Duane's good humor. At the island some folks got out for lunch (not everyone was testing for the bigger trip) and the rest of us ate in our boats. After precisely half an hour, Joe called for us to head back and once again sprinted off. This time the group spread out, some people showing signs of wear. When a container ship appeared on the horizon, Joe sped up to pass in front of it. The rear guard stopped to wait, effectively separating us into two groups.

My training told me to stay together, safety in numbers. But it wasn't my group and I had a test to pass. If I dropped back it might be a sign of weakness. Would I be judged unfit to join the expedition? Pedro had the same concerns and we talked in hushed tones, trying to figure out the right thing to do. Duane solved the problem when he announced he would drop back and make sure everyone made it home safe. He didn't need to prove anything, but his choice told me all I needed to know about him. I would go on to do many longer, harder trips with Duane over the years, and he proved himself a worthy companion every single time.

In the harbor the lead group stopped to wait for everyone, people straggling in, Duane with the last paddler who looked exhausted. Even Joe was unenthused about practicing rescues, and he offered to schedule a session for another date. In the parking lot he complimented Pedro and I for keeping up so well in our plastic boats. He looked forward to seeing how we handled the rescues and rougher conditions. First test passed but more to come.

I missed the rescue session because of a scheduling conflict and asked Joe if I could make it up. He didn't have the time but said that if Duane checked me off it would be good enough. Duane lived closer anyway, and we scheduled a day of paddling and practice around Palos Verdes, the southern tip of Santa Monica Bay. We met on a warm day, just the two of us, and launched through the surf to paddle around the rocky coast.

There's often an adjustment period when paddling with new people, figuring out their skill level and speed, making sure you're on the same page and can trust them if something goes wrong. Five minutes after leaving the beach I felt right at home with Duane. As we paddled, he talked about past trips to the Channel Islands and I soaked up the stories like the bilge sponge behind my seat. I spoke about my teaching experience and the newfound sport of kayak polo. We paddled close to the rocks, taking an occasional small breaker and calmly surfing in and paddling out; we both rolled multiple times to cool off.

"When do you want to see my rescues?" I asked.

"That won't be necessary." He had seen and heard enough. I was in.

o——o

The final roster for the trip totaled six; Joe and Duane, me and Pedro, and two San Diego paddlers Jeff and Rebecca. Duane had done the first leg of the paddle before, so he planned to take the ferry and meet us on the island. He was in it for the new sections, the places he hadn't paddled yet. For me and most of the others it was all new. The rest of us camped on the beach at Gaviota, up the coast a little ways from Santa Barbara, the night before launching.

Joe brought out charts and described bail out points and compass bearings. He double-checked his GPS and listened repeatedly to the marine forecast. Joe was a planner and the details were half the fun for him. The rest of us wrapped ourselves in warm jackets against the damp air, shared some stories of past trips, and hoped the wind would die down by morning.

I didn't sleep much that night, and at four a.m. I heard others begin to stir. Pedro clicked on his headlamp, awake with the same excitement. Time to get ready. Our boats were pre-loaded, but we had to break down the tents and stow the sleeping bags. It took four people to carry each of the loaded kayaks to the water's edge; they weighed close to two hundred pounds with food and water for a week, and all our camping and paddling gear. We stumbled on the loose sand, feet not yet awake. The light breeze chilled us in our paddling clothes as we listened to the latest forecast on the weather radio. A mechanical voice called for sun and warmth, bringing moderate winds late in the day. We'd be fine if we beat them to the island. No time for dawdling.

We gathered around the boats and turned off our headlamps to adjust to the ambient glow from the campground behind us and the city down the coast. The lights of the oil platform five miles out to sea confirmed the lack of fog, but the water was as black as the sky. The surf hit the shore in a muted rumble, small waves rising out of the dark to break on the sand. Everything set, still we hesitated. The unknown lay before us quite literally.

Joe launched first, charging into the void with his usual determination. We followed one at a time, me going last. Impossible to time waves I couldn't see, one broke in my face. Not enough energy to stop me, but more than enough water to soak me through and salt my mouth.

Once clear of the surf we gathered up. Each boat wore a glow stick on the stern, a faint light to mark our presence in the darkness. Joe lit up his deck compass with a small, waterproof flashlight and we followed him out to sea.

San Miguel was our destination, the westernmost of the islands. It lies twenty-six miles due south from Pt. Conception, the turning point of the coast and renowned for challenging conditions. The prevailing winds come from the west and get funneled into the gap between the mainland and the islands. San Miguel takes the brunt of the weather and this leg was the most exposed of the whole affair. Halfway across we'd be four hours of hard paddling from the nearest land.

We passed the oil rig at dawn, the fire atop its tower burning off natural gas like an everlasting candle. The sun lightened the day and I relaxed, more confident in the group and myself. I had feared my plastic boat, the only one in the group since Pedro had purchased a new composite boat for the trip, would hold me back, but we hit our desired pace and I kept up without a problem. The bulk of the Santa Ynez Mountains faded into the haze behind us before the small ridge of the island broke the flat horizon in front of us. Endless water in every direction. This was the adventure I wanted, out on a big ocean with nothing but my skills and companions to stave off disaster.

We paddled for hours, reaching a meditative state of rhythm and efficiency, with rest stops every hour to snack and use a pee bottle. Near the halfway point we saw a hint of land, a brown smudge directly in our path. It took a half hour before we trusted our eyes enough to declare it our destination. The relief of seeing our target was muted by the realization we were still several hours out. We each took a compass bearing in case we lost the island to fog, and Joe kept his GPS running as a backup, but we no longer worried about turning back. Forward was the fastest way to safety.

Dolphins crossed our path repeatedly, and a whale spouted in the distance. My shoulders burned with the constant effort, my hands raw from the drying salt water on the paddle shaft. It was hard work and beautiful and painful and easy and long. Joe and the San Diego contingent preferred to paddle in their own world, but Pedro and I enjoyed our usual rambling conversation. Kayaking can be a strange mix of solo activity and group effort. We all counted on each other for support in an emergency, but each person manned their own craft and everyone had to do the same amount of paddling. A team of individuals, connected by proximity more than anything, with separate motivations and different styles. Somehow it works.

When the shore approached, the rest of the group sped up to meet it, but I slowed to savor the moment. Several long days lay ahead, and the weather could change at any time, but I knew it would work out. I had made it this far; I could go all the way.

We enjoyed the sun and sand before hiking up the steep trail to camp. A leisurely afternoon and early dinner the reward for our effort. When the sun dropped below the island's crest, we were already asleep.

The next day dawned clear and calm. We had talked about hiking to the end of the island where the largest rookery on the west coast holds over seventy thousand seals and sea lions during breeding season, but with conditions like this, we could kayak over there. A rare chance to circumnavigate the island.

Duane showed up on schedule and joined us as we pulled away from the quiet beach. Our boats were as light as our spirits, our camping gear left ashore, and we circled San Miguel under bright blue skies, staying well clear of land to avoid disturbing the large and boisterous mammals sunning themselves and weaning their pups.

At that furthest tip of land we came across a fishing trawler pulling crab pots. They were amazed to find kayakers in such a remote place, and after a friendly conversation they filled an empty hatch in Jeff's boat with several freshly caught crabs. It seemed only right that nature provided a bounty to reward us for our success, and when we gathered around a picnic table for dinner, much laughter echoed into the starry sky.

The next day and our next leg took us to the south side of Santa Rosa Island and a remote beach, the only island where camping on the sand is allowed. The paddle went by quickly, only a short crossing between the islands that felt tame after the long void we crossed to reach San Miguel. After landing, a large splash caught our attention far out from shore. Ninety feet of sleek blubber exploded from the surface and crashed down with a gigantic splash reminiscent of the icebergs dropping off the glaciers in Alaska. A fin whale breaching over and over. Another sign nature approved of our progress.

After that we crossed to Santa Cruz Island, the largest in the chain. Nature decided to test us with a thick fog and unexpected currents flowing against us. It was my turn to navigate and I spent three hours paddling hard with my head down, eyes fixed on my deck compass, the needle swinging wildly as the sea bounced me around. No longer a meditative state, this was pure concentration and effort, the others dependent on me to find the south tip of the island without meandering and increasing our distance.

Nature relented, satisfied with my effort, and lifted the marine layer to reveal the island right where it belonged. I uncrossed my eyes and a wave of pleasure rippled through me as my muscles lost the tension they had held. I had never paddled so far and in such conditions with only a compass to guide me. Another success. Only seven hours of hugging the shoreline to go.

We covered thirty-five miles, the longest day of the trip, and pulled into the harbor on Santa Cruz Island late in the afternoon. Only one leg remained, the shortest one at that. Duane checked with the ferry that was anchored offshore—he had done this part before and didn't need to repeat it. The ferry had room and left in half an hour. Jeff and Rebecca were satisfied as well, claiming victory had already been achieved. But Joe was determined to complete his dream trip. He hadn't spent years preparing to visit four islands to be satisfied with only three. Pedro and I agreed (though we had only been dreaming of it for a couple months).

We saw half the team off and enjoyed one last dinner over the camp stove. Joe felt the effort of the long day and headed to bed early. Pedro and I stayed up until darkness revealed the lights clustered on the mainland. Millions of people lived over there, clogging the highways on their way to work each morning, fenced into their own back yards, occasionally going to the beach to sit on the sand without even noticing the pristine islands that sat just out of reach. How lucky was I to be on that island, to experience nature on a vast scale with a small group of friends. Or was it luck at all?

My choices had given me the skills to complete such a trip. My search for adventure had led me to Joe and his ambitious plan. My buddy Pedro was always there to lend a hand and provide me with good company. Sometimes luck is what you make it, and kayaking made it very special indeed.

On the next day we paddled to nearby Anacapa (a brief stop to claim our fourth island) and then over to the mainland. The last crossing was only twelve miles, three hours of solid paddling that felt effortless at this point. We hit the shore and went straight to the burger shack, no reward or recognition better than a greasy meal and recounting the trip with friends.

As great as the feeling of accomplishment was, the knowledge of what it meant was better. My trip to Alaska hadn't included any route-finding. We stayed close to shore and could always see our destination. But the Channel Islands expedition covered far more ground and included extended open ocean crossings. If I could handle this trip, paddle that many miles in a day, plan a route and navigate by compass when land was out of sight, I could go anywhere. The world of expedition kayaking opened up to me. I had no idea what would come next, but I knew I would be ready for it, and that's what mattered.

Hiking my kayak into the Kern River

Chapter 9

HIKING OUT

M y life revolved around kayaking. I taught sea kayaking at the MAC, surfed on my off days, paddled the coast with Pedro. There was no long-term plan for the future, but always a plan for my next outing. I had left the world of management behind, discarded my pursuit of physics, traded in the dream of a solid career and stable life for one of uncertainty and low pay. It was far easier to lose myself in the moment on the water than to face deeper questions about the future. I pursued my passion, like everyone always says they wish they could, and I assumed life would reward me the way paddling rewarded me for constantly pushing myself and improving my skills. I didn't worry about failure.

When spring rolled around, the river called, offering more challenge and opportunities to prove myself. I felt comfortable on the sea, and my polo skills were coming along nicely, but I had a long way to go to master the river and knew it required immersing myself in the sport. I set a goal to become a competent whitewater kayaker by the end of the season. The snow melt would only last so long—no time to waste.

Up to now the hardest whitewater I had paddled was class II, beginner level stuff. Competent, to me, meant paddling class IV, with my eyes on class V (the hardest level there is) for the future. It was ambitious but attainable, and the Kern offered everything I needed. I started with the same sections I had struggled on a year earlier. Under Paul's excellent tutelage,

I soon handled them without flipping and graduated to more challenging class III.

That allowed Paul to invite me to run Brush Creek, a tributary of the Kern steeper than most class V runs but without the powerful hydraulics. His talk of granite slides and fifteen-foot waterfalls sounded way beyond my ability, but he seemed to think I could handle it. The tiny creek doesn't run for very long, and if I waited for more experience I would miss it completely.

"Give it a go," he said. "You can always walk out." The creek is only a mile long and the road never far away.

I trusted him and was rewarded with the wildest amusement park ride of my life, sliding over smooth rocks and dropping off little waterfalls into deep, calm pools. The largest drop came around a blind corner and Paul only told me to stay right and keep my nose up. I rounded the bend and the world fell away, but I did what he said and felt a moment of weightlessly as I flew off the lip before landing with a surprisingly gentle impact. If I had taken the whitewater bait before, the hook was now set well and truly deep in my skin.

As I progressed I met more boaters and found new people to learn from. Lee from Santa Barbara, who had learned to paddle from Paul back in New Zealand years earlier; Andrew from San Diego, another expert boater friendly enough to take me down my first class IV run; and more time with Gilbert whose cabin served as paddler's lodge and whitewater university all in one. Kayaking formed a community, the common bond simply doing something different from the masses. A strange and wild bunch, old and young, with corporate professionals and dirt-bag boaters. I fit in there somewhere.

The season developed nicely and the class IV sections of the Kern became my new home. Sure, I took a few knocks, swam a time or two, but I kept improving. I learned to appreciate the joy of river running, once again tapping into the power of water. There's a special feeling to timing a single stroke to drive into the current and glide across the river away from a hazard, or taking the proper angle down a rapid, hardly paddling at all, letting the river dance with the rocks and following its lead. I felt comfortable on the river—too comfortable.

I needed something to test myself on, something to spur more growth and development and keep me from complacency, and our Fourth of July trip set the stage. At Paul's initiation, a large group of people headed up to run the Tuolumne River just outside Yosemite. Time to get away from the familiar and try out something new.

There are two commonly paddled stretches of the river. One is the main 'T', an eighteen-mile wilderness run with lots of class IV rapids and one class V. There are no roads and only one trail out of the canyon. It's a popular commercial rafting trip that normally takes two or three days, but kayakers can do it in one. It's a classic; a testing ground for boaters in the state. The other run, right above it, is much harder.

Paul, Lee, and Andrew went early to run the hard stretch, and the rest of us joined them afterward to set shuttle for the class IV run. We camped in a grassy field as the day's paddlers talked of the giant rapids they faced and the close calls they had. I relished the stories, hoping that I could join their ranks soon. It made me want to prove myself on the easier run, show these experts that I had the potential to be like them, but I really wasn't sure what to expect.

In kayaking, like life, the familiar is always easier than the foreign. I was comfortable on the class IV runs on the Kern partly because I ran them multiple times. I knew the lines, the hazards, the way different water levels changed the rapids. The people guiding me down knew them even better and gave flawless guidance and directions. No one on this trip knew the T. It was new and exciting and difficult.

The first rapid offered multiple routes, all shallow and rocky, and our group came upon a raft pinned on a boulder near the end. Paul saw it in time to direct us around the additional hazard, but one of the other new boaters flipped and swam in the process. My nervousness ratcheted up a notch.

The next two rapids saw two more swimmers though I managed to avoid the holes and stay upright. I didn't know whether to feel good about my success or be worried that my turn was coming. The whole group settled down and we continued to negotiate one class IV rapid after another.

When we reached the Class V rapid, Clavey Falls, our group stopped for a snack and a scout, and I faced the crux decision of the day. The rest of the first-year kayakers chose to walk around, portaging the hardest rapid on the river. Our leaders, including Paul and Katherine, decided to run the main drop on the right. Was I ready for it? Everything had gone perfectly up to this point —I nailed the upper rapids and knew I was strong and capable. But Class V? That was for experts only, as hard as whitewater kayaking gets.

The Falls were intimidating, water dropping off a ledge into a maelstrom of rocks and currents, and the smallest mistake would lead to painful consequences. It frightened me, and I didn't know if I should fight past the doubt or fly away for self-preservation. I split the difference and elected to run the left side, an easier route but a solid Class IV nonetheless.

My stomach couldn't handle even a granola bar, and I elected to get it over with as the others watched. I pushed off the rocky beach and ferried across the calm pool above the chaos, but the extra adrenaline had me paddling hard well before there was a need so I overshot my target. I back-paddled to slow down and line up my route. The entrance rocks pinballed me down a chute so shallow my kayak scraped as much as floated. Everything sped by, the drop approached, the current swept me too far to the left. No time to correct, I flew into the air and landed sideways, instantly flipped by the reversing current. I rolled up just as fast, operating on instinct, and saw that I was clear of danger. I pulled into an eddy. I made it.

Katherine stood above me with a congratulatory smile which I genuinely returned. I looked back up at the rapid, the 'easy' line that I screwed up and the 'hard' line on the other side. I was happy to make it through but somehow disappointed in myself though not exactly sure why.

The rest of the run went without incident. I should have been thrilled. This was my goal for the season, and I had succeeded by any measure. Any measure but my own. Nothing less than perfection would satisfy me. I had sidestepped the true test of Clavey—hadn't even stayed upright. Part of me wanted that bigger challenge, something that would scare me and push my limits. Fate was only too happy to oblige.

After the Tuolumne trip, our group resumed weekends on the Kern, the only river within easy driving distance of Los Angeles. I had fun and felt comfortable, repeating the same stretches I had paddled all summer long, but the dissatisfaction remained.

One Sunday, as the shadows lengthened and the day's heat faded, I met up with Paul as he finished the Forks of the Kern, a Class V wilderness run as remote as the Tuolumne but with more and harder rapids. It was on my list for the following year, but I asked Paul if he thought I could handle it now. Never one to hold someone back, he said with a smile, "Give it a go." That became the plan for the following Saturday.

The flow on the Kern had been dropping for weeks as the snow in the Sierra melted away, and it sat at an easy level when Paul accepted me. But a heat wave hit mid-week and flows doubled by the weekend. The high water generated faster currents and larger, more powerful waves. Paul still thought I could handle it even though his smile wasn't quite as big when we met to set shuttle. The addition of Katherine, Lee, and another strong boater meant lots of support, and we left a car at a trailhead midway through the run in case I needed to hike out. A reasonable, if not reassuring precaution.

The first challenge on the Forks was getting to the river, a two-mile hike carrying a forty-pound kayak down a dusty trail cut into the canyon's steep side. In spite of our early start, the heat made the walk a sweaty, miserable slog. My shoulder ached and I tried dragging the boat along behind me, but it kept sliding off the side of the trail, threatening to pull me over the edge. The uneven ground hurt my feet in river booties not designed for hiking, blisters growing with each step. I arrived at the river exhausted, dehydrated, and nervous as hell—not exactly in the best condition to kayak the hardest run of my life. But no way was I carrying my boat back up that hill. Paddling was my only option.

Paul assured me the run started easy and I'd be fine. Cool water splashed my face on the first rapid and washed away the fatigue of the hike, but the tension in my body made my paddling tight and forceful, not the fluid grace the others exhibited. The rapids were well within my skill level, but fear of the unknown had me fighting the river instead of working with it. Each stroke, every move, took maximum effort, leaving me out of breath when the first big rapid appeared: Upper Freeman.

We pulled into an eddy at the top and Paul described the line. Straight down the left between two rocks, then farther left around the coffin rock at the bottom. Lee went first to show us how it's done, but got pushed right and disappeared behind the first set of rocks. He reappeared paddling hard, inching his way left of the final rock to safety at the bottom.

"Hmm," Paul said, lost in thought. "Well then. Guess I'll give it a go."

With no hesitancy in his paddling, he peeled out of the eddy and charged straight through the rocks before the same thing happened to him.

I had my breath back but lost my nerve—if those guys had trouble, what chance did I have? Katherine assured me it was fine, no matter what happened. With dread, but resolved to face my fear, I floated out of the eddy and between the first rocks.

An unseen current pushed me right, same as the others, but I didn't react fast enough and it flipped me over against the coffin rock. I set up to roll but paused until I cleared the rock. The rough stone pressed into my shoulder as I waited. And waited. Eventually I realized the rock wasn't moving because I wasn't moving. Confused and running out of breath, I pulled my sprayskirt and swam.

"Swim to the right!"

Katherine's voice hit me the same time as fresh air. I followed her instructions blindly. Paul and Lee quickly arrived to tow me to safety and retrieve my gear. The water, recently snow on a mountaintop, sucked out any residual body heat from the hike and left me shivering on shore. No big deal, I reassured myself. That kind of thing happens all the time in kayaking. Just unlucky.

In the back of my mind I knew the run only got harder from here.

At the next big rapid, Lower Freeman, we got out of our boats to scout—no one wanted more surprises. The normal line against the wall on the right led to a gigantic hole that intimidated everyone in the group, but the same high water that made the usual route scary created a new opening on the left. Same as the last rapid, it was a straight shot between rocks leading to a large drop at the end. This time I watched from shore as the others ran it with no problem.

Determined to push on, but with the same sense of dread, I walked back to my boat as the others waited below. I slid my feet into the cockpit and stretched the neoprene sprayskirt to seal me in. Even that took more effort than normal. I slid off the sand and splashed water on my face to get ready for the inevitable dunking to come, the current slowly accelerating me toward my doom.

My kayak bounced off barely submerged rocks and my paddle pulled against the bottom as much as the water. I hit the gap and flew off the drop, much taller from this angle than when I stood on shore. At the bottom, the water caught the tail of my boat and pulled it down. I braced as I went vertical and clearly saw the blue sky framed behind my orange kayak. Prepared to roll, I miraculously landed upright, through the rapid and into the pool where the others cheered wildly. Too stunned to laugh, I looked back upstream. A slow smile crept onto my face. Maybe I'd be all right.

I survived the next couple of rapids, my confidence pulling me through and my body working to capacity. My skills were fine but my strength dwindled. I swam again at Needlerock Falls, another rock interfering with my roll. As I shook uncontrollably on shore, Katherine pulled out an extra thermal layer from her dry bag and pulled it over my head, dressing me like a helpless child. No longer a peer, I was someone who needed to be looked after.

It took several minutes to recover enough to paddle. Another rapid, another swim. No rock to blame this time, I simply lacked the energy to roll, exhausted from the failed effort to stay upright. More warm clothes, snacks shared from the group, and a switch to Paul's more stable kayak followed, but to no avail. I tipped over more frequently, unable to handle anything but flat water.

Worried about our pace, we pushed on as fast as possible. I walked around any significant rapid, too tired and weak to carry my boat over the rocky ground. As I struggled past giant boulders and through bushes of poison oak, the others ran the rapid, and then one of them walked up to run it again in my kayak. No longer just a nuisance, I had become a liability. Slowing down to help me put everyone at risk of getting stuck in the dark.

But there was no alternative, the canyon walls too steep and undergrowth too thick to hike out. The only trail wasn't until the halfway point. My brain registered all this and part of me felt guilty, but any real thought was beyond me. In survival mode, going forward was the only way out.

After a million rapids we reached a beach where a small trail climbed the steep hillside. The escape route, they told me. A car waited at the top with the key tucked under the rear tire.

"Just carry your kayak up the hill and drive down to meet us at the take-out."

I nodded and collapsed onto a small strip of sand; heat seeped into my body and made me drowsy. Paul repacked his boat with the gear I wouldn't need, leaving me a lighter shell to carry up the hill. Katherine refilled my water bottle from her own supply while Lee joked to cheer me up. They rushed to get back on the water, the day waning and lots of hard river miles between them and their destination. I understood and sat up to wave feebly as they paddled away.

Left alone, I lay back and stared at the blue sky, no orange boat blocking my view. Birds chirped, water splashed, and a light breeze carried the scent of the forest. No more rapids to face, no more rocks to hit or swims to survive. The ground beneath me solid and safe. I closed my eyes and took a long moment to appreciate the peace before acknowledging my day was far from over.

I stood and shouldered my boat, stumbling under its weight, and my relief at being on land soon changed to resentment for the terrain. Each step took conscious effort, and my paddle served as a cane. The trail started steep and got steeper. Soon I dragged the boat instead of carrying it, with frequent breaks to suck air, sip water, and curse my life. Eventually I tossed my paddle ahead and used my hands to scramble after it. Loose dirt slid beneath me and fatigue made me clumsy, losing a foot for every two I gained. I didn't know how long the trail was, how much time it would take to climb out of the canyon, or where I was in the world. I moved forward because there was no other choice.

At times the path was too rugged to drag my boat. I tied a rope to it, climbed ahead, then hauled the boat up hand over hand. The blisters on my feet expanded and new ones formed on my palms. My legs cramped and my arms trembled. The sun burned my neck raw. The boat got heavier and heavier, and I hated it for failing me. I wanted to cut the cord and send it crashing down to the river for the watery burial it deserved. I didn't. The failure was mine; I let it and the others down. This was the price of my overconfidence, and I wasn't going to fail on the hike. I yanked on the rope and lodged the kayak against a tree, clambered up, and repeated the process again and again.

After hours of incremental progress, the path met a gently sloped jeep trail. The rope became a harness and my kayak a sled as I walked on, watching each step because the effort to lift my head required strength I didn't have. My water bottle long since empty, I rejoiced at the slight relief when the sun fell behind the hills. When the car came into view a hundred yards away, I considered leaving the boat and driving back to pick it up. I leaned on the paddle, so close to the end but unable to think clearly enough to make a decision. Drop the boat? Drag it? In the end, it was simpler to stick with the status quo. I put my head down and trudged on, not stopping until I slumped over the car, the cool metal as refreshing as the day's first slap of whitewater.

The car held soda and chocolate, but I restrained myself to small amounts, my body and stomach too empty to handle much of either. It took two attempts to lift my kayak to the roof, my friend once again, a trusted steed that had served me well many a paddle. I checked my tie-down several times, running my hands over the straps and pulling in every direction to confirm the tightness, knowing enough not to trust my brain in my exhausted state. The drive down the winding road consumed my last reserves of energy, leaving me spent when I arrived at the takeout the same time as the paddlers. Finally, I could turn myself over to the care of others.

They were as happy to see me as I was to find them. Their adventure had continued with bigger rapids and more swims, but everyone was safe now, and we all had new stories to share the next time we gathered around a campfire. With mixed feelings of exhaustion, relief, disappointment, embarrassment, joy, and satisfaction, I handed the keys off and slept in the back seat the whole way home.

The river humbled me that day, but everyone gets humbled at some point. In the end, it wasn't my success at running Class IV that made me a whitewater kayaker that season, it was pushing myself to failure, then pushing more to overcome it. The level on the Forks dropped the next weekend, but I had learned my lesson. It would wait for another season, and I'd be better when I came back.

Chapter 10

HIKING OUT AGAIN AND AGAIN

As I grew as a paddler on the river, I continued my progression as an instructor on the ocean. When the head of the kayak program at the MAC moved away for a new job, he asked me if I wanted the job. The fact that all the other instructors simply assumed I would take over made the choice to accept an easy one.

It was still a part-time job with low pay, but more responsibility and more creative control. I helped revise the curriculum taught at the MAC and introduced new courses and new ideas about paddling in rougher conditions and on longer trips, even inspiring some fellow instructors to train for a crossing to Catalina Island. It felt like a perfect fit. Additional hours as a dockmaster at the facility and guiding backpacking trips on occasion supplemented my income. I was an honest to goodness outdoor professional, with the growing debt and lack of a future that comes with.

I also transitioned from student to teacher in whitewater, helping Paul with a large beginner weekend to start the season. In what was to become a tradition, we brought together as many experienced paddlers as we could scrape up and offered to train new boaters for just the cost of renting equipment. Modeled after the way New Zealand clubs work, the idea was to create the next generation of boaters and avoid the barrier to entry that commercial instruction and purchasing gear entails. It was a way to give back, to foster a community that paid off with more boating friends and good karma on the river. It also created one hell of a large group of kayakers to manage and teach on the river.

The first day we all stayed together, paddling a class I stretch on the Kern below the canyon, the very same stretch of water I started on. It felt good to know enough to give advice to others, but also a little stressful leading people down rapids. I felt very comfortable teaching on the ocean, where I was in complete control, but the river was a more challenging environment and uncertainty in my skills created worry in my teaching. The responsibility for someone else's safety always weighs heavier than concern for your own well-being. But Paul oversaw things on the water, and new mother Katherine sat on shore with the baby to offer support and suggestions. Everything went fine.

The second day posed a conundrum. Some of the students were ready to move on to more challenging stuff, but others needed a second day on the easy water. Paul thought I could handle the advanced group since it was small and some other intermediate boaters would go with me. He stayed with the larger group, and as usual I trusted his faith in me and put aside my doubts.

The best class II run for us was the same run below Lake Isabella that had hooked me on the sport years earlier. Excited and nervous, we drove up through the canyon, stopped to look at the scary class V rapids, and set shuttle on our little stretch. With three newbies on the trip and four experienced boaters, we had a good ratio. Of course, I was the only one who had done this run before, so it was up to me to describe the lines and show the way—final responsibility fell on my shoulders.

Some students swam on the first half of the run and I stayed tense the entire time. In spite of being relatively easy whitewater, a fair amount of wood washed down and got stuck on the rocks, creating strainers that could catch a kayaker (or swimmer) and pin them under water. Most rivers get flushed clean during the spring run-off, but being right below the dam meant this section rarely saw anything but minimal flows. On edge the whole time, worried about the consequences of a mistake, I stopped the group in the eddy above the biggest rapid on the run.

With private property on the only accessible side of the river, we had to stay in our boats—no scouting from shore. I knew the route, but the big drop came around a blind corner, and eddies in the rapid were small and hard to catch. I explained the move, a simple left turn and then straight down the drop, before positioning myself in one of those little eddies halfway down where I could signal the group. The two strongest paddlers followed and gave me the okay sign after making it to the bottom. The beginners came one at a time, with the final experienced paddler mixed in between for support. Everything went according to plan, and I followed the last person in the line, bouncing down the rocky drop only to find chaos in the pool below.

Two of the three beginners swam, as did one of the experienced folks. Boats and paddles floated on the water, and people kicked toward shore where most had gathered. I clipped an empty boat with my towline, grabbed a loose paddle, and shouted instructions for who to chase down what. Everyone responded quickly and the mess sorted itself out in no time. I pulled onto the rocky beach to assess the situation.

The beginners were fine, but the experienced boater hit her head when she flipped. She sat on shore with a circle of people checking on her. I hopped out of my kayak and joined the worried contingent.

One of the other boaters, certified in wilderness first aid, took charge. I had taken an EMT course years earlier, but wilderness medicine is a whole different ballgame. EMT's put people in ambulances and alert the hospital to what's coming their way; wilderness medicine involves treating people in places where it takes the professionals too long to arrive. I watched and listened but let him conduct the evaluation.

Head injuries are serious things, the risk of spinal cord injury always a concern. He kept her head immobile to be safe, even though she could talk and walk just fine, only complaining about a whopper of a headache. EMT protocol would be to call for a helicopter and tie the patient into a backboard. That sounded like overkill and wilderness protocols allow for a spinal assessment to clear the person to move. He performed the exam with good results: no tingling, no motor problems, no point sensitivity. Everything seemed fine. He okayed her for moving around, but she wasn't up for kayaking and we needed a plan to evacuate her and get everyone off the river.

A nearby house meant a nearby road, private property no longer a concern in a medical emergency. I split the group, the medic and beginners stayed with the injured woman and the rest of us paddled downstream as fast as we could to retrieve the cars. By the time we reached the vehicle a gentleman in an old pickup waited for us. He lived in the house and had seen the group walking the injured woman to the road and offered to help. Our friends rested on his porch while he drove down to meet us and show us the way back to his place, a snaking maze of dirt roads that would have taken us hours to navigate.

Our patient felt much better and we all shuttled back to the put-in and the rest of our vehicles. She wanted to head home and sleep it off, but I insisted she go to the local hospital to get checked out. While I sat in the waiting room I had time to reflect on my first experience as a leader on the river. Yes, people swam. But that happens all the time in this sport. Yes, there was some chaos. But I gave good commands and everyone did a great job helping out. No one likes a crisis, but it's nice when things work out in the end.

My balloon popped when they brought me back to see the patient taped down to a table with a large brace on her neck. She broke her C-1 vertebrae though managed to avoid any spinal cord damage. But the slightest wrong movement, a little piece of bone cutting that all-important lifeline, would have meant paralysis or even instant death. All from a little spill on class II whitewater. It doesn't matter how well you lead, bad things still happen. And when they do, it doesn't matter how well you handle a situation, the outcome might still be bad. It's a heavy responsibility and one to be prepared for. I helped her notify her friends and arranged to get her vehicle down to the hospital in Bakersfield where she'd be transferred. She had months in a brace with metal bolts drilled into her head and a year of physical therapy ahead of her. In the long run she was fine, but I never saw her on the river again.

The week after the incident, I led beginners down another stretch of whitewater. Back on the horse, I worked with Paul to learn more about being the one in front. How to choose your angles and start everything earlier so less skilled boaters can follow. How to anticipate problems and where to position yourself to respond. Not just on the easy stuff, but on class III and IV whitewater. We set up a rescue practice day, simulated boat pins and people stuck on strainers. I signed up for a Wilderness First Responder course—no more passing off the hard decisions to others.

I wasn't interested in being the one in charge because I enjoyed the responsibility, but because I knew I had the skills and abilities to handle it. My time as a teacher in front of a class, and as a manager in charge of an office, had given me plenty of experience running the show. I was no longer an aimless kid but a man in his thirties comfortable with authority and little patience for ineptitude. I hoped to never need my training but knew it was probably just a matter of time. The Tuolumne once again played the role of test piece in my paddling career.

The Fourth of July trip had become an annual tradition. The river ran off dam release throughout the summer and offered a refreshing change from our normal routine. July was late enough in the season for people to have developed the skills to handle the river, and a three day weekend gave enough time for the long drive to reach it. This year we planned to do a day on the main T and then visit some other rivers in the area. I still wasn't ready for the class V upper section, and no one else could work it into the schedule anyway. A comfortable run down a class IV sounded good—and it would give me a chance to compare myself to last year's version. Could I make it down without flipping at all?

The group was the normal mishmash, some polo players, some UCLA people, but no Gilbert or any of the San Diego crowd. Paul led as always, but with Katherine watching the baby, I was second in command. We had three first-timers on the T, and one more along who decided to sit out the first day of the trip and wait for easier rivers. At the put-in, we ran into a couple kayakers from San Francisco running it for their first time and Paul invited them to join us. We hit the water as a large group, a good mix of skilled and learning boaters on a warm summer day. It was nice to help with the leading, but nicer to let Paul be in charge.

The continuous class IV at the beginning challenged the new folks and a couple people swam early on, but nothing too bad until the last rapid before our planned lunch stop at Clavey Falls. It was a class IV rapid, but not particularly hard or fearsome, named Evangelist because it was 'hole-y' (kayakers and rafters like to give rapids clever names, like 'The Hole that Ate the Donner Party' or 'Pinball'). Paul went first and I was sweep, coming after everyone to make sure they all made it through. A group of rafts charged into our midst and I pulled out of their way, not wanting to get run over. When I reached the bottom of the rapid, the rest of the kayakers were on the side of the river, half of them out of their boats and circled up around a girl. Déjà vu hit hard as I paddled over.

Roslyn sat on the ground and one of the guys held her head still. Blood flowed freely from her forehead and dripped off her chin. Everyone was hesitant and this time I stepped into the middle of things. Paul reported she flipped and hit her head on a rock. She didn't remember it. In fact, she had trouble remembering much besides her name. She didn't know where we were or how she got there.

Fresh off my wilderness first aid training, I assumed responsibility and went through the textbook evaluation. The blow to the head and short term memory loss clear signs of a concussion, the inch long gash on her eyebrow required stitches but wasn't life threatening. Again, EMT protocol said call the helicopter and wait. I was all too aware of the consequences of moving her with a possible broken neck. But five miles into an eighteen-mile run, deep in a wilderness canyon, there was no cell coverage or quick way to get the helicopter to us. Even if we paddled out and made the call, it would be hours before they could reach us, maybe not before nightfall, and who knew if they could land in the dark. She might be bleeding into her brain and that required immediate surgical intervention. We had to get her to help as quickly as possible. There was no nearby house this time, no road to bring in a car. Nothing but bad choices.

I didn't want to do anything. I wanted someone else to make the decision. There's nothing fun about taking charge of a life or death situation. But no one else was eager to do it. I had the training, knew the procedures, and knew I was good at them. It wasn't about what I wanted or was afraid of, but about what was best for the injured girl who needed our help.

I evaluated her spine and found no injuries or indications of damage. I repeated the procedure and confirmed my results with Alex, one of the UCLA paddlers who had been a classmate in my first aid course. We both agreed she showed no signs of a spinal injury and we could move her if necessary. We just had to decide if that was necessary. Everyone had a thought on the matter, but as the highest certified medical professional at the scene, the decision was mine.

I put it off for a moment. Clavey was right around the corner, and commercial rafters often camped there for the night. We flagged down a passing raft and they offered to take her to the campsite—they were headed there anyway. Roslyn climbed aboard for the short ride with the rest of us following in our kayaks, Paul towing her boat.

The camp was full and that meant many people offering even more opinions. A vacationing nurse said to keep her still and go for help, a former EMT said she could probably handle a raft trip the rest of the way out. But no one offered to take over for me. They all had advice and suggestions, but the decision, and the burden of it, was still mine.

Ironically, Roslyn herself was a med student and wanted to keep paddling, but her memory loss invalidated her opinion. But it did show she felt strong and capable.

I decided we had to get her out as soon as possible, but how? The raft guides would have taken her down the river to safety but the river level was dropping—the dam release we floated on only lasted a few hours, if you got behind the bubble there wasn't enough water for a raft to make it down. Luckily there was a single trail that exited the river canyon and it started right across from the campground. Three miles of a steep climb in the scorching sun, but it ran to a road near civilization. The closest and fastest option. Decision made.

I went with her, my duty as the head caregiver. Alex, hiked out with us; he had similar training and was the strongest guy in the group. Evan, the random kayaker we met at the put-in, ran the trail ahead of us to make the call for an ambulance. The others paddled on to get to the vehicles and drive back for support if needed. Everyone willing to do whatever necessary to help out.

The hike was surreal. Roslyn's memory lasted for about five minutes then reset.

"Where are we?" she asked.

"We're hiking out of the Tuolumne River," I answered.

"What happened?"

"You flipped and hit your head."

"Am I okay?" She touched her bandage.

"You're doing great, just keep walking."

"Where are we?" she asked again.

The conversation repeated over and over. I asked her questions to interrupt—"What's the last movie you saw?", "What rotation are you doing in med school?"—and determined she had lost a year of her memories. Completely gone. She stayed in excellent spirits and never got tired, perhaps she just forgot about the heat and pain. Alex and I dripped sweat and silently cursed each start of the cycle. It was slow torture, but both of us knew that things could turn much worse at any moment: heat stroke could set in, Roslyn could lose consciousness, we might have to perform CPR. If I could have held my breath for the entire climb I would have.

At the top more déjà vu waited in the form of an old pickup with a friendly local who came to give us a ride. She took us to her house where Evan waited with help on the way, already having called 911. We sat Roslyn in the shade and gladly accepted some cool water. The highway patrol showed up with the paramedics and I let out the breath I had been holding. I should have learned not to relax too soon.

The paramedics took Roslyn inside to evaluate her. They came out five minutes later, said she refused care, and climbed in their ambulance and drove off. I watched them leave in disbelief. The duty to care was back on me. She needed to get to the hospital and I had to figure out how to get her there.

The highway patrolman was kind enough to drive Roslyn and me to the nearest town—his regulations didn't allow him to take us any further. The town didn't have a hospital but it had our friends. They had made it off the river and drove back up to meet us. One of the women offered to take Roslyn and me to the nearest hospital, an hour away. More traveling, but this time inside an air conditioned SUV instead of trekking on foot in the summer heat. More comfy, but I didn't relax.

Another tense waiting room session ended with the call to come back and see the patient. This time she was sitting up and smiled, a sign that the ordeal was over. They ran an MRI and everything was fine. Her memory had returned and the pain medication made her giddy. She wanted me to hold her hand while the doctor stitched her up. It was the easiest thing I did all day, and possibly the most rewarding.

They cleared Roslyn and the three of us headed back to our group camp spot. We pulled in at midnight, but everyone woke up to greet us. After a day of anxiety, the wave of happiness and relief that came from the group washed me clean of my worries. But with the medical situation resolved, the paddling situation still needed fixing. Roslyn's boat, my boat, and a couple others lay on the side of the river, halfway through the run. Someone needed to drive Roslyn back home. I handed the logistics over to Paul and crashed hard on my sleeping pad. It's nice to have competent people around to take over when you're done.

The next morning some of the group paddled from the put-in while myself and others hiked in to the boats, including the nervous paddler who hadn't kayaked the day before. Paul figured that if he put in below the big rapids the rest of the river was within his skills. Everyone met at Clavey and proceeded from there.

The day before I had planned to run the class V line on the right side of Clavey, ready to push myself and prove my abilities had improved from the year before when I snuck my way down the left. After the stress and strain of the day before, I didn't even look at the right side. I went left, no desire to push or prove anything. I made it through upright this time.

Evan and his girlfriend sprinted ahead, anxious to get off the water and back home. The rest of us progressed slowly, with Paul leading the newbie who hadn't been with us the day before. The poor guy was in over his head and on one of his swims he broke his paddle. Paul traded out paddles, using half a blade to canoe down the river and leaving me to show the rookie the lines, once more in a position of responsibility.

It was another long day, but we finished with no emergencies. I enjoyed the paddling even though I focused entirely on looking after others. It was okay, I had the skills to do it. After all, that's what had been done for me when I needed it.

No one wants bad things to happen, but sometimes that's when you learn the most. Not only about myself, but I had learned a lot about the people who surrounded me. Everyone did what they could to help. They stayed calm, offered good suggestions, and put the group's needs before their own. Everyone supported my decisions and stayed positive throughout the extended drama. These were good people, and I fit in right alongside them. Not a bad place to be.

It didn't dawn on me until the ride home that I hadn't flipped once all weekend.

Aiming for the sky on the Kern River

A whitewater kayak in the surf

An arch on the Channel Islands

Triple Drop on Brush Creek

Kayak polo tournament in Los Angeles

The Lost Coast of California

Whale breaching in British Columbia

Totem pole in Cha'atl, Haida Gwaii

Camping on the river

A fine boof in Ecuador

Chapter 11

ECUADOR

Becoming a teacher and leader on the river helped my paddling skills; becoming a mentor gave me a new paddling buddy and a lifelong friend.

Alex, who helped me hike Roslyn out of the Tuolumne, managed the Outdoor Adventures program at UCLA, which ran the backpack trips I sometimes led. Technically he was my boss, but I was several years older and he was just out of college. He rock-climbed, backpacked, and mountaineered, and even paddled in the ocean a bit, but didn't have my years of management experience in the business world. We got along fine, but our differences created an underlying tension that kept us as associates rather than friends.

That changed when he started whitewater kayaking on the beginner trip earlier that year, the one I helped Paul lead. Alex attacked whitewater kayaking with the same passion I had when I started, and the two of us began to boat together regularly. I put him through the paces on class II and III, eventually working up to class IV. It was his first time on the Tuolumne when the Roslyn incident happened, proving he could be trusted to help when things went sideways. We explored the rivers of California together and the more challenges we faced the deeper our friendship became.

After the end of a season in California, Alex decided we shouldn't wait idly by for the rains to come and snow to melt but instead travel somewhere the rivers still flowed. We looked south and Ecuador popped onto our radar. It's always warm, the Amazon never dries up, and prices are low. And it has a well-established kayak scene with a guidebook detailing the runs. Arrangements were made.

Alex invited several others, always looking to include more people in the fun. He talked our friend Danny into coming, a UCLA undergrad just getting into class IV but conveniently fluent in Spanish. He roped in an old college buddy, Dave, who lived and boated in Colorado, and Dave's friend Chris, a solid boater out of Seattle. We even had a doctor, a Kern River local named Frank. None of us had done any whitewater kayaking outside the States, but we had all travelled extensively. A good mix of skills and experience, and a great group of guys to paddle with.

While everyone got sick at some point on our trip, I bested them all by getting ill on the flight down. I arrived in Quito with a chest infection and nasty cough, made worse by my asthma and the city's elevation of nine thousand feet. Unable to sleep, I was in a daze of misery as we explored the city and caught a bus over the Andes to Tena, a small town on the edge of the Amazon and the epicenter of kayaking in the country. Our rental kayaks awaited us at our riverside hotel and I took a nap while the others planned the first paddle.

The Upper Misahualli was the epitome of Ecuadorian kayaking, a boulder garden outside town that starts in a rainforest as a difficult class IV and gets easier as it descends toward civilization. Danny arranged a ride to the put-in with a local taxi driver accustomed to hauling kayakers around in his little pickup. We tied the boats into the back with our safety ropes and five of us squeezed into the cab. Danny rode on top of the boats like a bargeman working his way down the river, ducking branches and swatting mosquitoes while hanging on for dear life. He was young enough to do that sort of thing.

Recovering from my illness, I barely managed to carry my boat the short distance from truck stop to the water. We launched and paddled a couple hundred yards before getting out on the opposite side to scout the first major rapid. Trees blocked the main channel and low flows cut off the alternative, so we walked around it. More hiking meant more coughing and wheezing and I stopped for a long breather at our new starting position.

As they all waited for me, Frank, the doctor, decided to put in and run the last drop of the rapid we portaged. It was a tricky ledge that looked like it would suck you back into a sticky hole if you didn't clear it. In a group of strangers, everyone was hesitant to take too big a risk, or to make suggestions for someone whose skill level they didn't know. Alex was our leader on shore, but he wasn't as experienced on the river as some of us. Chris was a super strong paddler but was recovering from a knee injury and didn't know anyone besides Dave. I was just happy to set my kayak down and close my eyes while Frank hiked up for his run. Everyone held their breath and waited to see what would happen.

Frank tried to boof, a technique as you go over the lip of the drop where you pull on your paddle to shoot your boat out and beyond the bottom of the mini waterfall. Unfortunately, he didn't make it far enough and our assessment proved correct— the water sucked him back in. He took a solid beat down, unable to escape the hole and eventually swimming out of his kayak. With the rest of us right there for safety, we quickly got him to shore and retrieved his gear. On the one hand, swimming wasn't a great way to start a trip. On the other, it broke the tension.

Frank joked about his bad line and complained that no one got a picture of the carnage. Someone offered to take pictures if he ran it again, and Frank blithely agreed. This time as we all waited there was laughter, and several cameras were held at the ready. Frank had an ugly line again, flipping at the bottom, but managed to roll up and paddle over to us. He declined a suggestion of a third run and we all got in, our spirits a little lighter.

Everything went smooth the rest of the run. The scenery was incredible and vastly different from California's mountain forests, with giant kapok trees rising out vibrant ferns below and colorful parrots darting in and out of the deep shadows above. The kayaking improved, with near-continuous rapids full of smooth boulders that created endless routes and little danger. The short paddle took up what little energy I had for the day, but I ended with a smile on my face.

The takeout was in a little village with a single bus stop. When the old diesel-spewing beast arrived, Danny and Dave climbed the ladder on the back as the rest of the guys lifted the kayaks up to them. Before they could tie things down the vehicle took off, eager to maintain its schedule. The guys up top clung to whatever they could grab, holding the boats to keep them from flying off, and we all made it safely back to Tena, stopping a block from our hotel. Shuttles in Ecuador often proved more dangerous than the rivers.

One day in the books, we headed out to a local eatery for dinner. On the way we spotted more kayakers – their pale white skin and polypro clothing dead giveaways they weren't local. They were from the U.K. and had been in town several days already. We joined them for dinner and cervezas, and they shared valuable information on the rivers and more. They invited us to the Napo River Festival the next day, where kayakers could get a free shuttle to run the Jatanyacu, a class III big water river with lots of play spots. How could we refuse?

The festival, a combination of local celebration and tourist attraction, featured small crowds and a lack of organization that left me confused (though the new cough medicine Frank helped me acquire may have contributed to that as well). Somehow we ended up in the back of a stakebed truck with our kayaks, a dozen other paddlers, and a ten-foot anaconda, all headed to the river and the first annual Ecuadorian Freestyle Kayaking National Championships. The snake wasn't paddling—just along for the ride.

Freestyle kayaking, or playboating, is the kayak world equivalent to the skate park. Instead of going downriver, you find a single feature, ideally a nice river wave, to perform tricks on. It starts with surfing the wave, but moves on to flat spins, cartwheels (vertical spins), and loops (a front flip). In competition, judges score each paddler on the difficulty and style of the maneuver, much like gymnastics without the dismount. None of us had much experience as playboaters, but

Chris and Frank stepped up to represent the good ol' U.S. of A. Our new friends formed Team Scotland, and a single local paddler, Juan, rounded out the competitors. The only thing missing were judges.

Alex and I were conscripted and taught the scoring system by a festival representative who didn't speak English. Through a lot of gestures, some sketchpads, and translator work from Danny, we kind of figured out what we were doing. Team Scotland joked about bias but didn't volunteer to help—they were happy enough to stay in their boats and play around. Luckily the finals came down to one of the Scots, our very own Chris, and the local Juan. Even better, Juan clearly dominated the round—no protests were filed when we awarded him the gold.

After a very short award ceremony, everyone got back in their kayaks and headed downriver to enjoy the rest of the run. Normally a big volume river, the unusually dry weather had left it low, making kayaking a bit more technical but still relatively easy. Easy for class IV kayakers, but not so easy for the newbies we ran into half way down the run.

Three more local guys had decided to give the river a try, with almost no kayaking experience and borrowed boats a decade past their prime. We found them on shore preparing to launch after their umpteenth swim, eyes big and fearful in any language. We offered to help them down in spite of our complete lack of knowledge of the river. For instance, we didn't know that at these low flows one of the rapids became class IV, with a river-wide ledge hole that eats kayakers for breakfast.

I led the group right into the beast and barely pushed through it myself, turning back to see three people stuck in the hole together. Chris and Dave hung on to flush out and roll up, but one of our new friends swam again. The rest of the group saw my mistake and avoided the meat of the hole, and we all quickly helped the swimmer to shore. He was oddly in good spirits and said something about enjoying the company in the hole. Sometimes all it takes is knowing you aren't alone in your difficulties to make you realize you can overcome them.

With a little more caution we finished late in the day with no more swims and three new Ecuadorian kayakers in the world. As the sun faded and the temperature remained constant, the festival became a party and everyone had something to celebrate.

With good feelings and good karma, our next run was the most remote of the trip, the river Anzu, and its shuttle didn't disappoint. An hour of driving dirt roads in another small pickup, Danny now enjoying the ride up top, found us in the middle of the jungle, path blocked by a group of men next to a loaded flatbed truck stuck in the ditch. They wanted us to pull them out, an impossible task for our little vehicle, but they wouldn't let us past until we tried. Pointing out the obvious futility—their truck outweighed ours by thousands of pounds—did little to persuade them to move, perhaps due to the bottles of rum being passed around their group. Eventually our driver hit the gas, nearly losing Danny and running down several staggering workers in the process, but getting us free from the situation.

The final descent to the river was a mile of loose rocks and after dropping our boats the driver insisted we ride back up the hill with him to provide the weight he needed to get traction and make the climb. It also meant we had to walk back from the top, but we couldn't say no to our savior. Shuttles in Ecuador are quite the adventure.

All that time and insanity brought us to a trickle of a stream that rumor claimed held a rapid stretching uninterrupted for seven miles. We hoped it was worth it, but the meager flow made the first hour more boat-bashing than kayaking, scraping over rocks and dragging our boats through the shallows. Our spirits sagged until a tributary entered and doubled the flow, renewing our optimism.

With the new water, we approached a drop that looked significant from above, too steep and boulder-filled for us to see what lay at the bottom. Physically strong and capable again, and eager to do my part, I paddled to the lip to get a better look while a couple of other guys tried the other side. In my rush I got too close, my boat tripped on an underwater rock I didn't see and spun around, sending me down the drop backward and blind. I held on as I accelerated and banged off rocks, bracing to stay upright. My tail bounced sideways and I stopped dead, pinned against a mid-stream rock and using my hand to keep me from flipping over. My head was above water but current poured over my boat and locked me in place. I was stuck.

I waved to the guys above for help but couldn't see any response. I was okay as long as I could hold myself up, but with one hand holding my paddle I knew the other arm wouldn't last long. Below me lay a pool of deeper water, safety if I could reach it, but the only way I could get off the pin rock would require two hands and probably flip me over. My newly returned strength faded fast and I made a decision. I threw my paddle toward the pool, freeing up another hand to push off the rock.

It worked, but I flipped as expected. Before I could set up for a hand roll, my body hit another rock. My boat slid over the rock and the pressure increased—my body pushed into an underwater wedge, trapping my arms against my side and leaving me firmly stuck upside down. Panic gave me a burst of strength, I yanked my hands out of the crack and reached for the top of the rock, shoving with everything I had to extract my body and free myself. The water slid me across and into the pool, still upside down but no longer trapped. Any thoughts on hand rolling long gone, I frantically reached for the grab loop to pull my skirt and kicked like a wild animal to get free.

A hand reached down and pulled me up. Standing in two feet of water, Alex lifted me clear and steadied me as I gasped and sputtered. He and the others had found another way around the drop and came back to help me. If I had held on while stuck sideways they would have been able to walk out and pull me free; if I had remained stuck in the wedge, Alex would have been there me almost immediately. I was only under for ten seconds and suffered no injuries. The facts said it wasn't really a near-death experience. My mind thought otherwise.

I had swum out of my kayak a number of times before, been stuck against rocks and unable to roll, caught in holes and recirculated, but this was the first time my mind regressed to sheer survival instinct and it took a while to climb out of it. That surge of adrenaline gave me the strength to escape, but now it left my heart pounding and body shaking. The group sat me down and patiently waited for my intellect to return.

A few minutes on solid ground and the report that my paddle couldn't be found brought me back to reality. We had a spare along, but the thought of losing my trusted paddle upset me—anger a better feeling than fear. I scoured the rocks of the rapid and eventually found the paddle wedged in the very same underwater crevice that tried to hold me. A simple reach into the water pulled it free and switched my brain back to paddling mode.

This was the beginning of the seven mile rapid, one drop after another with no pools in between, only the occasional eddy to take brief rests. I didn't lead any more rapids, nor try to scout close to the edge, but I made it down cleanly. Some moments felt completely normal, just kayaking down a cool river within my skill level. At other times, panic rose randomly to make me doubt every ripple of water or boulder blocking my view. I greatly enjoyed the rapid and hated it at the same time. When we got off the river in a warm rain, I wasn't sure if I wanted to ever get back on again.

The next day we moved up mountain to a new base in the town of Baeza, and while the other guys got in a quick run on the local river, I took the afternoon off and slept in the hotel. We only had a couple days of paddling left and I needed a break to think things over. More accurately, I needed to stop thinking about my pin and let my mind get back to normal. Nothing had actually changed—I always knew kayaking had dangers and it was a fluke of bad luck that happened to me. My team had responded well and everything worked out fine. I knew all that, but the fear remained. With no enthusiasm, I forced myself to paddle the next day.

Getting back on the water saved me. We hit the Cosanga, one of my all-time favorite runs. It had boofs galore, four- to six-foot ledges with nice clean lips allowing you to launch yourself into the air and land gently below the hazards. My paddling was the sharpest of the trip and everyone had a great time. All back to normal.

Only it wasn't. The last day of kayaking for the trip followed, a relatively easy run to get to the lodge where we'd drop off our boats. I flipped in the biggest rapid and repeatedly missed my normally reliable roll, but held on and kept trying, eventually rolling up after a long time under water. I didn't know if I should be proud of my eventual success or worried about my difficulties with a skill I thought I had mastered. I walked the next big rapid, not sure if I should test myself here. When I flipped again at the bottom of an insignificant drop, I couldn't roll up even though I floated in completely calm water. Another panicked escape left me confused and shaky the rest of the day. Dropping my boat off and knowing I didn't have to face any more whitewater relieved me more than anything else on the trip. This wasn't normal at all.

We treated ourselves to a night at a resort before heading back to Quito to fly home. We soaked in hot springs outside our cabin and swapped stories we all knew and were a part of. Everyone, me included, called it the trip of a lifetime, the best whitewater, the best people, the best experience. I truly believed that, but I also knew that something had changed for me. My mental approach to the sport needed adjustment, and I wasn't sure what boating would mean for me when I returned home.

Friends in the darkness

Chapter 12

CREEKING IN LOS ANGELES

I came back from a dry rainforest to a wet desert. Los Angeles experienced a series of storms that flooded local streams and created rare opportunities for kayaking in the local hills. One doesn't normally think of whitewater in Los Angeles, but both the Angeles Crest and Santa Monica Mountains offer plenty of gradient. Water is what's normally lacking, but a couple months after my return the ground was soaked and the creeks primed to run.

In that time I paddled one weekend on the rain-fed Kern and realized a few important things. First, my roll worked perfectly as long as my head stayed out of the whole affair. Second, the familiar class IV of the Kern felt easy after the challenging rivers in Ecuador. In fact, I longed for the uncertainty and challenge of paddling an unknown stretch of whitewater. Finally, if I waited too long to push myself again, I might never do it. I needed to get back out there on something hard before I settled into the comfortable and tame, and the rainy weather provided the chance.

Paul came through with an invitation to go creeking over the weekend with him and Andreas, a friend of his from Germany recently moved to L.A. and itching to get in some difficult whitewater. The Arroyo Seco in Pasadena sat on top of the list of options, an incredibly steep run through ten miles of National Forest before ending at the parking lot for NASA's Jet Propulsion Laboratory. We needed one more rainstorm to make it runnable and Mother Nature obliged on Thursday night. Game on.

Creeking differs from other forms of whitewater kayaking in both the steepness of the run and low volume of the water. Gradient is measured by the number of feet a river falls over the course of a mile, with class III normally around thirty feet, class IV around fifty, and class V over one hundred. The Arroyo Seco falls an average of one hundred and seventy feet per mile, with some stretches over two hundred. While most rivers flow with a volume of water of at one thousand cubic feet per second (cfs) or more (the Colorado runs at least ten thousands cfs through the Grand Canyon), creeks are much smaller. The Arroyo Seco can be run down to one hundred cfs, or so claimed our only source of information, an old website from a kayaker who had run it ten years earlier. A lot can change in ten years.

We met at Andreas' house early Sunday morning, his wife kind enough to help us set the shuttle. We loaded the kayaks onto their Volvo, and I jumped into Paul's old Saturn for the trip to Pasadena. The website guided us to the JPL parking lot but it was closed for the weekend, and we ate crucial daylight hours searching for a lot we could access. We found a park downstream to drop off the station wagon and all piled into the Volvo, careful not to bury the baby seat in kayak gear. Andreas' wife would drop us off and head home, leaving us with no other option than reaching the take-out to get home.

The drive up the Angeles Crest Highway climbed steadily and I craned my neck to see any sign of river below, but the forest was too dense. We stopped at a day use picnic area where the creek was a tiny trickle of water heading away from the road and toward a giant waterfall. We loaded the kayaks onto our backs with makeshift straps to hike the trail that followed the stream, planning to start kayaking when a tributary joined in below the falls.

The many picnickers enjoying a sunny day between storms watched us pass in fascination, clearly doubting our sanity. Part of us knew they were right. It was almost noon and we had a two-mile hike to get to the boatable stretch of creek. Once in, the gorge was fifteen hundred feet deep with no trails out, fourteen hard river miles to reach our car at the takeout. In spite of the day's hot weather it was still early in the season and the sun set by six pm. Our chances of making it out before darkness were slim.

We knew that but we continued anyway. There's often a time when the cautious route is to turn back and return another day when the odds are more favorable. But no great achievement was ever reached by playing it safe, no personal wisdom gained or soul tested by the discretion part of valor. When all reason screams to retreat the important thing to know is what will happen if you try and fail. If you accept that risk and those consequences, then you push on and live with what may come.

Paul got sick of carrying his boat and decided to paddle to the top of the falls and walk around from there. The gradient here was three hundred and sixty feet per mile and it had half the water it needed. Andreas and I kept walking. We gave Paul beta—information on the route ahead—and he kayaked at our pace. Five minutes in he cracked his paddle when it wedged between two rocks. By this time in my career, I knew omens could be taken any way you liked. Maybe we were in for a series of bad luck accidents, or maybe our bad luck had been used up. We took the optimist view and soldiered on, with Paul paddling mostly on his good side.

We all hiked around the falls, a pair of drops totaling a hundred feet and clearly not safe for kayaking. We continued walking until we reached the addition of Bear Creek, bringing in enough water to make kayaking a reasonable choice. We all geared up and put on.

Perhaps the most important rule to creek boating is that you never paddle past what you can see. To do that, you need to make sure you can always stop before going over a blind drop, so you paddle from one eddy to another, small bits of counter-current that allow you to pause and look downstream. In a small creek most eddies only have room for a single kayak, so it's one person at a time as you pick your way down. It takes skill and precision and a sharp focus, and it takes time. Content to let my more experienced elders lead, we advanced slowly.

The run was steep but not too difficult. My nerves faded and I enjoyed the paddling, what we could manage. We got out to scout frequently and walked around many drops because of a lack of water or a tree blocking the route. In an effort to increase our pace, we started to leapfrog, with the lead person hopping out to look and directing the others where to go. This rotated our front person and I took my turn finding the way, feeling good and determined to contribute to the group.

Out front in a particularly long stretch and boating well, the river disappeared a hundred yards ahead and I scanned for an eddy, signaling the others to stop. No eddies in sight, my speed picked up and the blind corner approached. More scanning, still nothing. I needed to stop and only saw one option. The banks on either side were within reach and I snagged a tree root, swinging my boat sideways and pinning myself against a rock. The water pushed on my sprayskirt and I held myself upright, unable to move without sliding back into the current and unknown danger.

It was the exact same situation as the pin in Ecuador. This time I didn't panic or try to free myself but waited for help to come. My signal gave the other guys enough warning to stop and get out. Paul ran down to me and reached out from shore to hold my boat while I stepped out into the shallow water. Andreas gave me a hand and Paul pulled my boat in. Lesson learned and reinforced, we all scouted the corner and saw it was good to go. I passed the lead off to Paul and followed with a clear head, Ecuador behind me now. Experience and faith in your fellow paddlers goes a long way toward peace of mind.

We held the pattern until we reached an unnamed waterfall, this one only a dozen feet tall. It looked like it might be okay if you hit it with speed and a good boof stroke, but the lead in was shallow and rocky and none of us had confidence we could make it clean. We chose to walk around, but that was easier said than done. The walls were steep, vertical on one side with a narrow ledge on the other. Not something to attempt with a boat on your shoulder. We tried to climb higher for an easier path.

With the most climbing experience in the group I led the way up two pitches, tying a rope off for the others to follow and hauling the boats up behind us. The higher we climbed the less likely it appeared we'd find an easy route. After some sketchy handholds and close calls, we retreated back down to the creek. We climbed around the narrow ledge and set a rope along its course to slide the kayaks along. Easy enough in the end, but the whole process took a couple hours.

By the time all three of us and our equipment were safely on the downstream side, the sun had set and twilight was fading. We put on and paddled as fast as we could. The river was harder here, portaging the rapids meant wading in chest-deep current and leaping from rock to rock. Too dark to tell water from stone, we admitted defeat and called stop. Time for plan B.

This is where preparation and understanding came in. We took our time, eating the extra food we brought and filtering more water for the hike, pulling on the extra warm clothes packed in drybags, turning on our headlamps—Andreas even pulled out a pair of hiking boots he has stashed for this very possibility. We were well prepared.

Our boats tied off safely above the creek and out of sight, we began the climb up to the trail our map showed on the south ridge. The trail followed the river and would take us to our car. It was plan B, but it was a solid plan.

That doesn't mean it was easy. With no trail, climbing the steep canyon walls meant fighting through manzanita and grabbing poison oak to keep from sliding back. Four hours later, fifteen hundred feet higher, we hit the trail around midnight. Not a single harsh word passed between us, nor any recriminations for who had gotten us into this mess. In fact, we laughed and enjoyed our misery as much as we had the paddling. The only curses were saved for the vegetation.

Still several miles from the parking lot, Paul pulled out a cell phone to call Katherine and pass the word that everything was fine, but we'd be home a little late. The hike was all downhill from there, with the lights of the city twinkling below us, bright enough to drown out the real stars in the heavens. We even stopped for pictures.

The exertion kept us warm in the cool evening and we took the opportunity to scout the bottom of the run as we walked along. By four a.m. we reached the parking lot, only to find a locked gate and Paul's Saturn inside. Even that didn't get us down.

Not content to wait until sunrise and a city employee to let us out, we built a ramp from stones and carefully drove Paul's old wagon with one wheel on the ramp and one on the dirt, sliding between boulders placed to prevent exactly that. We all commented that our timing was perfect—we got out just ahead of rush hour. At six a.m. my head hit my pillow, lucky enough to have the day off from work. The other guys weren't as fortunate, but at least they had happy wives to come home to. Part one of the adventure complete.

During the week we watched the flows. The Arroyo Seco fell, but it still had enough water to boat. We scheduled part two for Saturday. The amazing part wasn't that we hiked back in to retrieve our boats and paddle out. The thing that stands out in my mind about that day was the fact that Lee, Paul's friend in Santa Barbara, hiked in to join us.

In our small kayaking community, word of our exploits traveled quickly. At the polo session on Monday evening, the one I barely woke up in time to attend, Paul and I repeated the story several times. We talked about the heavy kayaks and blazing heat on the hike in, about breaking paddles and getting pinned, about scaling sheer cliffs and walking through the night. We showed the scratches on our arms and rashes on our hands. We smiled and laughed as we told the story and half the people pitied us and the other half wished they'd been there. Lee was one of the latter.

He fit right into the adventure, carrying his kayak while we hiked down the river to our boats. After the first falls, he paddled while we scouted for him, the entire group progressing seamlessly. When we reached the second falls, the one with the hard portage, we jumped right into rigging a line to send the boat around and made it past in no time. We reached our boats and the four of us continued down the creek.

With half as much water the paddling was harder, not in a class-V-challenging sort of way, but in a how-do-I-get-down-this-without-bumping-off-a-dozen-rocks sort of way. Short stretches of fun whitewater existed, but overall it was more work than pleasure. We even had a bonus half mile hike to get around a diversion dam, but we took it in stride and kept moving. In spite of our early start and efficient travel we once again got caught by darkness. This time it was only a mile from the car and a flat trail followed the creek the whole way. We made it to the Saturn, parked outside the gate, before midnight.

When I think of the fun moments that paddling has brought me, the incredible views and exotic locations, one of the first images to spring forth is Andreas and Paul standing arm in arm posing atop a ridge overlooking the lights of a city of ten million people. The closeness and camaraderie we found on the Arroyo Seco is something you don't get from the picnic grounds or a short hike to the falls. It sets us apart from those who never leave their concrete environment; it makes the hardship and struggle more than worth the effort. I overcame my fear and doubt and re-found myself through kayaking, and nothing would take that away again.

The week after the Arroyo Seco (Part 2), Paul, Andreas, and I paddled Piru Creek, a run that starts along Interstate 5 thirty miles north of UCLA before dropping into a remote canyon that few people ever see. We started at dawn and covered the eighteen miles, including three across the lake at the end, by two in the afternoon. No pins, no swims, back home by dinner. Sometimes it's good to get it right.

Photo Krisztina Peterfy

Thick in the action

Chapter 13

KAYAK POLO WORLD CHAMPIONSHIPS

After Ecuador, in between those L.A. creeking missions, I paddled in the pool, playing kayak polo twice a week with the regular group. The pool was safe and helped me get my focus back on paddling and away from rocks and danger. My skills had improved to the point I rarely got pushed over, even by Paul, and the level of competition in our local group no longer challenged me the way it once did. That meant comfort, a good thing when recovering from a scary incident, but also a trap that prevents growth and development. As I always did, I looked outside my comfort zone for more ways to test myself that would force improvement. I decided to try out for the national team.

The Kayak Polo World Championships happen every other year, with the top twenty-four teams in the world receiving invites. The United States team barely makes the cut, often getting a wildcard invite because the Europeans who dominate the sport want to encourage its growth across the pond—or maybe they like bringing us over to beat up on Americans for a change. A small sport in this country, with only half a dozen clubs that played competitively, kayak polo lacked organization, and after every Worlds the national team disbanded and disappeared for a year before someone would start it back up to prepare for the next championships. Such lack of consistency was a large reason for the poor performance on the international stage.

Before I made the team, I set about fixing the system and began immediately after the previous Worlds, working with my friend Patrick, a UCLA teammate and aspiring national player himself, to develop a system to keep training in the down years. We divided the country into two regions, East and West, and each picked their own coach and held their own training camps. At the U.S. National Championships the year before Worlds, the two regions would play and the winner would represent the U.S., ensuring a core group of players with more experience working together to build skills and foster teamwork.

That meant I had to first make the West region team, and then we had to beat the East, the main source of national players in the past. At this stage in my polo career I played in the top division and competed with the national team members, but I was far less experienced and my skills were below theirs. Experience takes time and skills take practice—I focused on the skills. Instead of just attending our twice weekly pool sessions, I organized weekend trainings with the group. I went out before work for sprints and conditioning drills. Patrick and I got together to work on passing and ball control. I added evening strength training to build my speed and endurance. No longer a mere hobby, polo became a sport, a serious, competitive endeavor that deserved my sweat and tears (or maybe that was just water splashing me in the face).

By the first training camp I saw improvement, now able to match up with the competition and believed I could make the team. I doubled down on my efforts and moved up the ladder, at least in my mind. Our coach, Clyde, was a hard-ass who rarely praised anyone and never told us where we stood for fear we'd be content.

"You're all crap," he said, and then got in his boat and put us all to shame—he was a former World Champion from England and still played at that level. "You'll have to do better to beat the East."

They had hired their own British coach, Clyde's old nemesis, and it wasn't just our pride and reputation at stake—

Clyde wanted to win at least as much as we did. I liked having someone push me and Clyde liked to push, so we got on well.

Our west coast squad consisted of me and Patrick from L.A. and several players from San Francisco, the very same ones who impressed me at that first tournament years earlier. Everyone put in the time and effort and we all improved. When Nationals came I was happy, though not surprised, to be one of the starting five. The east coast had enough players to divide into A and B squads and we played them both. We whipped the B team by an embarrassing score. Their A team didn't do much better, and it was painfully clear who deserved the represent the U.S. Clyde even told us we did okay. It was a year away, but I made plans to attend the World Championships in Amsterdam, representing my country and playing kayak polo against the best in the world.

Somewhere along the way my goal to make the team changed—no longer satisfied with being competitive against American caliber players, I needed to compete against the rest of the world. I needed to be the best, even if such a goal was impossible. My workouts intensified, my focus narrowed. I gave up whitewater kayaking for a year—it interfered with training—and stopped teaching sea kayaking. I put everything into polo.

Maybe not coincidentally, at the same time I gave up on my dream of making a living through kayaking. For years I had worked at the Marina Aquatic Center, and when the center manager had resigned, I was told the position would be mine. But there was a hiring freeze. Then a new department director was hired. Then the process to hire a manager became complicated and political. Then someone else got the position and my years of struggling to survive in Los Angeles on a mishmash of part-time jobs and responsibilities seemed pointless.

I had no career, no savings, no way to pay for the travel required to be on the national team. Instead of figuring out what I wanted and needed for the rest of my life, I pushed away life's concerns and made kayak polo the only thing that mattered. A mindless office job paid for a new carbon/Kevlar polo kayak and who cared if the work sucked my soul dry.

Each day I woke up before the sun and drove to the marina for a conditioning session on the water. Even Los Angeles is cold that early in the day, my breath fogging and body shivering in a short sleeve lycra top as I walked down the dock. No longer young enough to completely recover from the day before, I'd swallow a handful of Ibuprofen and grimace through my warm-up, paddling until steam rose off my bare head. Then came sprints and intervals until I couldn't breathe; then a little more. No time for a cool-down—a quick shower, breakfast in the car, and into the office by eight. Work through lunch to be able to leave by six. After dinner came strength training or games at the pool. Sleep came early and hard.

Weekends held more training or travel, often to San Francisco to work with the rest of the team. A six-hour drive each way for two full days of training left me exhausted for the start of the week. We even flew to Canada to play against their national team at a tournament in Edmonton in February (indoors). Life was simple and hard: do everything possible to become a better kayak polo player. No time for fun, friends who didn't play, or a life outside the sport. A ridiculous dedication to a silly sport that holds no fame or fortune, but somehow it made me content. When the team voted me captain, it validated my effort, but it was never a goal and came with a price.

It should have gone to Lance—he was the best player and had been to four World Championships—but he didn't want it. Captaining the U.S. National team was a huge honor, but it was also a lot of work. Something about competitive athletics makes grown men act like little children. People argued over everything, from plays on the pitch to where to get dinner afterward. Egos got hurt and tempers flared. Each and every person on the team was a good guy, and we all had the same objective, but it's the nature of the beast that conflict arises and emotions get the best of us. Our coach lived five thousand miles away and in his absence it was up to the captain, me, to wrangle the troops. Being one of the youngest and still the least experienced made my job harder. I just wanted to play kayak polo, but I knew Lance would play better without the responsibilities, so I took them on my shoulders. We headed to Europe for a warm-up tour leading up to the Championships in Amersterdam.

Our tour started on a sour note, a tune-up tournament in the Netherlands on a rainy weekend in July, camping next to the pitch in miserable conditions. After Clyde made us roll in the murky water to flush out the jet lag, I caught a bug and became feverish and chilled. The team played poorly and we even lost to the Great Britain women's team. That brought out more arguments and complaints about playing time and who to blame. Everyone was certain it was someone else who was the problem. Clyde went home for the week and left me to supervise. Unable to eat, puking while paddling, I spent all my energy trying keeping the team happy to no avail—even my choice for where to spend our day off was criticized.

The next weekend's tournament saw better results, with a win over Canada and good games against quality European teams. I recovered and played well myself, but the constant training and non-stop games took its toll on my weakened body—my shoulder hurt. Having suffered through rotator cuff problems from college tennis, I upped the Ibuprofen and pushed through it. We moved on to the World Championships in Amsterdam as ready as we were going to be.

The tournament opened with us against the home team—the favorite to win it all. The Dutch players towered over us on shore and paddled circles around us on the water, scoring at will. We were the Washington Generals to their Harlem Globetrotters. At half time even Clyde couldn't stop the yelling and finger-pointing. By the end of the game no one said anything. It was embarrassing and a stark reminder that I wasn't even close to being the best. Time to get ready for game two.

We faced Brazil, another opponent much better than us, but we played them close before eventually losing. Next we lost to a South African team that we realistically should have beaten. That became our pattern: play well against better teams only to lose in the end, play poorly against teams our own level to lose some more. We played great defense and stopped even the strongest teams, but our offense sputtered. Lance was our main scorer and he did his job well, but I was supposed to be his wingman and my shoulder didn't have the strength to shoot. I tried to create opportunities for others, but it felt like there was more interest in finding fault than finding a solution. We stayed close in every game and always had the chance to win, but a few small mistakes, a couple bad bounces of the ball, and we finished winless for the tournament and dead last in the standings. A very bitter pill to swallow.

The long flight home by myself gave me time to reflect. The truth is we didn't play well as a team and that's why we lost. I tried as hard as I could to work with everyone and my own play suffered as a result, but we never gelled. Everyone and no one was to blame. Personalities and egos clashed too much, sucking the fun out of what I had enjoyed most about polo: the team. I had lost tournaments before, been on teams shellacked by twenty goals, gotten schooled by better players, but always appreciated the experience because my teammates shared it with me. The group bond made victories sweeter and defeats bearable. Without that, losing just sucks.

But another truth is that we raised the level of kayak polo for our country even if the results didn't show it. Our team was far more skilled than the previous team (which also finished last). Not only were we better players, but we knew more about the sport and shared that knowledge with our clubs, raising the level of polo in the U.S. Our regional training system made it easier to get more people access to skilled coaching and increased the pool of players vying for the next national team. Our efforts hadn't been in vain.

Personally, even with the injuries, illness, and distractions, I tested myself against the best and proved myself worthy. Aside from the first game against the Dutch, I never felt outclassed. I kept up with the sprinters, held my position against players fifty pounds heavier, blocked passes, stopped shots, scored goals, and played at a World Championship level. All my hard work, the training and practice and dedication, even my struggles leading the team, accomplished something worthwhile. I put everything into kayak polo for two years and left nothing behind. No fans welcomed me when I landed, no congratulations came in from across the country, but I held my head high. My arm, on the contrary, hung limply at my side.

It took a month to get an appointment with one of the best sports surgeons in Los Angeles. He suspected a torn labrum, but the MRI was inconclusive. For a normal person that meant no surgery, but he was willing to do an exploratory operation to get a highly conditioned athlete back to the National Team as fast as possible. I thanked him but passed on the surgery. I was a former athlete, a retired kayak polo player. I only paddled for fun now.

A swimmer dropping into a hole on the Merced River

Chapter 14

HIGH WATER

Several months of physical therapy and no paddling followed the Kayak Polo World Championships, allowing my emotional wounds to fester and turning me into a serious grouch. No longer working in the kayak industry, with no polo to consume my thoughts and a job I hated, I began to wonder what the purpose to my life was. Was it kayaking? Shouldn't there be something more? I had no idea and let the water sweep away my worries.

Snow started to melt and the rivers began to flow. My therapist—physical, not mental—cleared me for paddling, and I soaked myself in the fun of kayaking comfortable rivers with good friends. My sunny disposition returned with the summer's heat, my life on hold until the season ended.

I brought everything great about whitewater kayaking together for our traditional trip to the Tuolumne River over the Fourth of July. This year everything was bigger and better: an overnight trip instead of one day, raft support to take more gear, over twenty people of all different levels and experience.

The river was also bigger but that wasn't better. Normal summer flows are one thousand cfs, that year we showed up to find the river over ten thousand cfs. Game changer. We gathered as a group to discuss the increased flow and evaluate our options. The commercial raft company next to us turned and headed home, too much water for them. A couple guys in our group, including Gilbert from the Kern and my old mentor

Paul, had boated the river at these levels and knew it could be done. Dave and Chris from the Ecuador trip had driven from a couple states away and were up for the challenge. I thought the high water sounded like awesome fun, but some of our kayakers were relatively new, and some of the raft passengers had never been on a river. At those flows, if any little thing goes wrong—and something always does in large groups—the danger is very real. The leaders debated what to do, the ones with the knowledge and experience to make the decision were the ones who could handle the river. None of them wanted to suggest backing down, and they all turned to me to make the final call—the captain by default.

I didn't want serious; I wanted fun. I suggested we skip the Tuolumne and head one river south to the Merced, less difficult and not as remote. The drive there went through Yosemite National Park, a treat for the out-of-staters. While some individuals were disappointed to miss out on the Tuolumne, everyone agreed it was the right decision for the group. My team was with me this time.

After a morning of sightseeing we reached the Merced, the road running alongside the river, providing escape if something went wrong. It also gave us options on where to start paddling—the farther upriver the more difficult the whitewater. The bulk of our party decided to start at the highway bridge, with a mile of continuous class IV before reaching the normal put-in and class III below. As most of us unloaded, some of the kayakers headed another mile upstream to run even harder rapids. That group consisted of Paul, Chris, Dave, and Alex, but also young Danny and his less experienced friend Rob.

I'd run that section before and remembered it as fun, but my shoulder wasn't one hundred percent and I didn't want any more stress, so I stayed behind. They had enough solid paddlers in the group to handle anything. At our put-in, the rafters rigged their boats and everyone took care of themselves, no one needing my help. I walked upstream to take pictures of the rapids, waiting for the kayakers to come down. I stopped next to a gigantic hole that would make a good backdrop for photos and enjoyed a moment of solitude.

My first indication the kayakers approached was a whistle, the signal for trouble. Kayaks came around the corner with no one in them, followed by a pair of swimmers in the water and the other kayakers chasing them down. Armed with only a camera, I helplessly watched the action unfold.

Paul and Chris bulldozed an empty kayak into a small eddy against a vertical rock face, Danny clinging to their boats. Luckily, he was an expert rock climber and hauled himself out of the water to safety. Dave and Alex chased after the second swimmer, Rob, who headed straight for the hole in front of me. Easy to avoid in a kayak, not so easy while swimming. I yelled to alert the rafters below—they had ropes to throw to the swimmer. Rob dropped into the hole and disappeared from sight, popping up a few seconds later thirty feet downstream and moving fast. Alex skirted the hole and continued after Rob, while Dave caught up to the empty boat and corralled it toward me. I grabbed an end and pulled it ashore, then checked in with Paul who gave me the okay signal. A little excitement to start the day, but it seemed under control now.

Dave told me Rob's paddle was missing, and I ran downstream to see if the others had found it, expecting to see Rob sitting onshore with the rafters. But no Rob, no Alex, and all three rafts were pulling away from shore in a hurry. I guess the excitement wasn't over.

I hopped in my kayak and chased after them. The river is continuous in this stretch—no eddies, no place to stop, and lots of rocks and hydraulics, some of them large and angry. I overtook the first raft, the least experienced of the bunch. They informed me that Rob hadn't caught any of the ropes and floated past, Alex right on his heels. All the rafts gave chase, but these guys had problems with their oarlocks and needed to stop. They beached themselves in the shallows to work out their equipment malfunction and I continued on.

I sprinted downriver, soon breathing hard and feeling the burn in my arms, my conditioning lost during my long rehabilitation. The big waves tossed me around and exploded in sprays of white, making it hard to see more than a few feet in front of me. In a lull I spotted the rafts a hundred yards ahead and realized I wouldn't catch them before the next big drop. It also dawned on me that they didn't know I was behind them. I was essentially kayaking alone on a high water class IV river I barely remembered. If anything happened to me, no one was there to help. So much for low stress.

The rafts made it through the drop and I followed their line, thankful for the guidance as I snuck between big holes. One of the rafts caught a small eddy against the shore and I swung in next to them to catch my breath. I had to yell to get their attention—when they stopped, the dog in the raft jumped out and sprinted into the woods, its owner right behind. Apparently the dog realized what a cluster we had going and wanted no part of it. Smart pooch.

The raft's captain thought the swimmer was still in the water but wasn't sure. I told them to stay put and send a second person after the dog—everything should be done in a minimum of twos. Don't let anyone else continue past alone, and we'd all meet up downriver somewhere. Time to get things under control. I dashed away, a little slower and more cautious this time.

Rounding the next corner, I found Alex swimming in the water next to his kayak, the raft far in the distance. What the hell? He grabbed onto my kayak, dragging his boat along, and we floated a ways before we found an eddy where he could stand. He had found Rob's paddle lodged in some branches along shore and tried to retrieve it as the raft helped Rob. But Alex got tangled in the branches and flipped, unable to roll when his paddle was stripped from his hands. I pulled out the breakdown paddle from my stern while he emptied the water from his boat, and we continued on together.

We found the final raft at the picnic area, the place where kayakers normally start their run. Rob was with them, a little waterlogged but no worse for wear. They also had Alex's paddle which had floated to them as they waited. Rob's paddle was still M.I.A. Alex and I joined them on shore, watching upstream for signs of life and hoping everyone would come through okay.

Eventually the rest of the team turned up together. The dog had been found by firefighters on the road and returned to the owner in the second raft. The first raft had fixed their oarlocks and made the rest of the rapid fine. Danny had gotten back into his kayak and all the kayakers joined up with the rafters, moving downstream with no more incidents. We took a long lunch break, a collective breather, and regrouped.

No injuries, only one missing paddle, and the hardest rapids all behind us. Not so bad. We geared back up to run the rest of the river, this time starting from where we should have begun the first time.

The rest of the day went well. Everyone was in good spirits, the river bouncy and fun. We surfed big waves and flipped to cool off. We stopped at a side creek and hiked up to find a swimming hole—not the river hydraulic kind of hole, but a pool of flat water surrounded by dark rocks and green trees. Splash wars led to chicken fights which led to sunning ourselves on the rocks. At the end of the paddle, Rob hiked along the river and found his missing paddle. We finished the day around a campfire, everyone sharing their perspective of the morning's chaos and laughing at themselves as much as anything.

If it had been a polo game, the morning would have been a butt-kicking. But that's the difference between competition and recreation, between losing a game and facing a setback. It's also the difference between men fighting for their egos and a group supporting each other against adversity. When bad things happen on the river, everyone comes together and turns it into a win. It didn't really matter if it was on a polo pitch or a wild river, I wanted to surround myself with people who not only enjoyed the same things as me, but also enjoyed them in the same manner. People who received as much pleasure from other people's successes as their own, who put the needs of the group before their own desires. How much pleasure I found in life depended more on who was by my side than where I went or how far I made it.

The next day some of the guys chose to paddle a nearby class V section of the Kings River. Again I chose to sit out the hard stuff. Along with the rest of the group, I drove up the canyon and watched the kayakers come through the major rapids. When Dave got stuck in a hole and eventually swam out, several folks jumped in to lend a hand, solving the problem as soon as it arose. I didn't have to say anything or even lift a finger. They had it covered. It was good not to be needed, and I enjoyed my role as just another paddler on the trip.

Chapter 15

DARKNESS AND LIGHT

When I left the UCLA kayak program for a desk job to pay for the World Championships, I figured it was the end of my professional kayaking career. Teaching didn't pay enough for a future, and I was retired from competition. I knew I needed to find my path, but in the meantime I had a job which paid fairly well and paddled for fun. Then one day, as I ate a sandwich at my desk and surfed the internet on my lunch break, I came across a job opening for a whitewater and touring program manager in northern California. Full time, with benefits. My dream job and one I was eminently qualified for.

Part of me was afraid. Afraid to move away from the city I lived in for the past fifteen years, afraid to leave the business world a second time to chase a hobby, afraid to leave my friends and start over at almost forty years of age. Afraid kayaking wasn't really my calling in life. Another part knew that nothing great is ever achieved by staying put and avoiding risk. I dusted off my résumé and within three weeks I had interviewed, accepted an offer, moved to Sacramento, and started work.

The irony of being back in the industry was that I was so busy kayaking for work I rarely got out for fun. I upped my certifications and became an Instructor Trainer (someone who certifies other instructors) on both the ocean and river. My job led to new contacts in the kayak community, and I learned so much more about the sport—about boats and equipment, about the economics of the industry, about different forms of kayaking. I lived near the epicenter of California's whitewater world and a short hop to an ocean much more dynamic than anything near Los Angeles. But it was really another desk job, more time spent on spreadsheets and phone calls than on the water. I just wanted to go paddling with my friends more often.

I got my wish when the economy tanked and my position was eliminated. Unemployment checks fueled a six month paddling odyssey. For the first time in my career, I was a true paddling bum, chasing flows with no responsibilities and no attachments. I ticked off new rivers and explored new coastlines. My skills improved and I could go anywhere and paddle anything I wanted. Every kayaker's dream.

I should have been ecstatic, but something felt empty. I enjoyed myself but missed the old joy of paddling, the appreciation of my own abilities and the world around me. Every day the sun rose into blue skies, grass grew a little browner, and rivers flowed downhill—the same as the day before. Paddling wasn't enough. I wanted a purpose, something to do with my life that felt worthwhile, but didn't know what it was.

Instead of spending my time in reflection or starting down a new path, I went paddling. It was expected of me. I filled myself up with greater challenges, ran harder rivers and bigger drops, pushed myself with the same attitude that carried me to the World Championships. My skills plateaued and risk became the only obstacle to advancement, fear replacing fun. My search continued.

Life on the road also meant an ever-changing posse of paddlers, finding folks from Canada to run Dry Meadow Creek, or a Colorado crew to tackle the Yuba. Good people, but transitory ones who came and went without any deep bond. I was normally the old man in the group, and my angst over my paddling career and lack of commitment to the moment separated me from the young dirt-bag boaters who shared my time.

My friends joined me when they could, and those days were the best, but after a weekend they returned to work while I continued on my quest for new waters. I felt myself caught between the kayak world and the real world, but kept paddling whitewater because it was there. Eventually the rivers dried up, and my journey brought me back to the Kern, one last whitewater trip before I switched focus to the ocean.

The upper Kern was out of water but the lower Kern, fed by the dam, had the perfect flow. I joined old friends for an easy day on the class IV run, everyone else in playboats while I paddled my creeker, the only boat I had with me. Play boats are short and low volume, designed for surfing waves and doing tricks. Creek boats are relatively long and bulbous, designed to handle difficult whitewater. My boat took the challenge out of the run, and I filmed and took pictures while everyone else played. We stopped for lunch at the standard portage, eating atop a rock overlooking the infamous Royal Flush rapid.

Early in my career I heard stories of people running the rapid in the good ol' days, but now everyone simply walked around it on the wide path created for that purpose. It was too dangerous to kayak. I had enjoyed the morning and should have been content with the many rivers I'd done and the good friends I had with me, but I still longed for the excitement and uncertainty I had when I first learned to kayak, right here on the Kern. I ate my sandwich and stared at the rapid until I saw a line—a route through the madness I could make in my kayak.

I announced my plan to run it, and in the silence that followed I heard the concern and doubt of my friends. But when they did speak, asking about my route or how I wanted them to set safety, they were supportive. They trusted me and respected my skill. It was my decision to make and I had made it. Enough said.

Royal Flush is tricky for several reasons. It starts with a pinch that accelerates the river, then widens only to crash into a large rock in the center. A second rock below creates a backed up hole, water piling and surging, unpredictable and dangerous. Going right of the first rock avoids the hole, but a sieve waits below—a narrow slot not wide enough for a boat (or body) to pass—and the one exit can only be reached through the confusing mass of water between the rocks. Getting left at the start requires fighting the main current, then running a six-foot drop into a sticky hole whose exit flows into a cave against the left shore. Stay upright and the hazards are navigable, but flip at any point and your life is at risk. That's why everyone walks around it.

I saw a route and paddled it in my mind. Come in hot with right to left momentum, use a stern pry on the left to slow down and change angle. Get as far left as possible in order to run the drop charging back toward the right, away from the cave. I knew I could do it.

Everyone rallied around the plan. A couple guys jumped in their boats below the rapid to help pick up the pieces if I swam. A couple more grabbed throw ropes and positioned themselves as close as possible to the hole and the cave. The rest of the crew got out cameras as Alex walked me back up to my boat. He asked me to talk him through the line one more time. He saw what I saw but asked, "Are you sure about this?"

I nodded, he patted me on the back, and I climbed into my boat. Once a decision is made, it's best to run with it and not let the doubt build up. The river rewards confidence and punishes indecision. I splashed cold water on my face and peeled out into the current.

The pinch accelerated me more than expected. My stern pry came too late and I didn't make it as far left as I wanted. A little hole grabbed my boat and I braced to remain upright. The next hole spun me around, heading backward into the big drop. No time to turn around, I tried to back-paddle. The big hole flipped me and the current under the surface flushed me out. I set up to roll but darkness swallowed me and my paddle hit something solid. I was in the cave faster than I could think.

I pulled my sprayskirt and exited my boat, my helmet hitting the ceiling while still underwater. My boat bounced against me and the current shoved us both deep against the back wall. Daylight shown from the entrance, but the force of the water made it unreachable. Down in the gloom, I groped for an exit or air pocket. Nothing. My lungs burned and I was stuck. All motion stopped and in the pause I experienced a moment of clarity.

I would die here if nothing changed. I accepted that inevitability and felt no remorse or panic. Risking my life gave me no thrill and no fear, chasing meaning on the river had led me nowhere. The emptiness I experienced couldn't be filled by the largest of adrenaline rushes. If this was my end, so be it.

Acceptance was not the same as giving up. Current tugged at my foot and I remembered one story of someone else running this rapid, getting stuck in a cave before swimming out a tunnel. With that faint recollection, and knowing that any movement was better than staying still, I pushed off the ceiling and let the current suck me lower, down into the depths. The pressure built as the walls pushed in on my sides, then I shot out into a deep, calm pool, the surface a bright light above me. Lungs empty, my life vest floated me gently to the surface. I closed my eyes and savored the peace; I would be all right.

I broke the surface and serenity with a loud gasp. Voices cheered and asked if I was okay, one of the guys sped toward me in his boat. Alex stood on the rocks and hauled me out of the water. Someone called out that my paddle floated past and everyone jumped to help. My inner calm vanished. What had I put these people through, these good friends of mine? How horrifying to watch me disappear and not know if I would ever return. I wanted to vomit, to cry. It was the most selfish act of my life and yet the only concern they had was for my well-being.

Apologies and thanks would come later—I assured them I was fine and asked about my paddle and boat. Without them I would be a greater burden to the group. The paddle was retrieved and the boat still stuck in the cave. I wanted to help in the recovery but Alex insisted I rest. They came up with a plan to lower someone from the cliff above to hook a rope to the boat and pull it out; an incredibly risky maneuver and I told them to wait. The thought of someone getting hurt saving my equipment made me feel worse. Luckily, the river took pity and spat out my boat, deciding it had already taught me my lesson and I was free to go on my way. With more help I emptied the kayak and we finished the run.

That was the closest I came to dying on a river, but it didn't mess with my head the way my pin in Ecuador had. I clinically evaluated my failed attempt and decided I only missed my line by about a foot. Just a little further left and everything would have been fine. As it was, I handled the bobble well and did everything I could to stay upright, even my decision to run the drop backward instead of turning around had been correct. Once in the cave I kept my cool and did all the right things, which is why I made it out. If I ran the rapid again, knowing the current better and experiencing the drop, I was confident it would go fine. I learned from my mistake.

But I didn't go back and run Royal Flush. I would have gained no sense of victory, found no joy in such an act. It would give my life no greater meaning, but only bring worry and possibly pain to those who care about me. In paddling difficult whitewater, injury and death are always too close at hand, a careful balance of risk and reward. I stepped back to find a new balance, a new reward that came at a lower cost. Life had more meaning than paddling though I still didn't know what that was.

Chapter 16

A LONG DAY OUT

After nearly dying on the Kern, I temporarily shelved deep thoughts on the meaning of life and my own mortality as I rushed to prepare for a six-week sea kayaking expedition to British Columbia. I had used the rivers to avoid thinking about life; I would use the ocean to avoid thinking about death. With several ambitious multi-day trips planned, I needed to get into long distance paddling shape and needed to do it in a hurry. Pt. Reyes offered a perfect training venue and the chance to complete an excursion I had longed planned but never got around to doing.

Pt. Reyes is a cape sticking out into the Pacific a short ways north of San Francisco, a block of land caught between the Pacific and North American tectonic plates. The whole chunk moves slowly north, about two inches a year—or up to twenty feet at once as it did during the 1906 earthquake. It lies on the San Andreas Fault, a cut in the earth mostly buried under Tomales Bay, a sliver of water separating Pt. Reyes from the mainland. For years I wanted to paddle around the cape, taking several days to cover the seventy-five-mile route. With lots of packing and prep work to complete for B.C., I shortened my sights: halfway around in a single day.

Making plans on the fly, I chose not to invite anyone along. Not many people would be up for a thirty-five mile day and have a Tuesday off to get it done. Besides, I was preparing for a solo trip so paddling alone made sense. I drove down the night before, my kayak atop the truck and my bike in the back for shuttle.

I locked my bike next to the visitor's center at Drake's Beach to await my arrival the following day and headed back to Tomales, scouting for a launch site. In my earlier plans, I expected to start from my friend's cabin on the east side of Tomales Bay, the closest access to the Point. But it would add twenty miles to the bike shuttle, so I needed to find someplace on the western side. The beach at the state park would have been perfect—if the park opened earlier than nine a.m. I needed to be on the water and paddling at sunrise to make this work. I settled for a turnout on the main road that never closed but added ten miles of paddling inside the Bay. Shorter bike ride but longer paddle. I definitely needed an early start.

Trip logistics set, I found a parking spot on a quiet back road and climbed into the bed of the truck for as much sleep as time allowed. A check of the forecast called for a small craft advisory the next day, winds predicted to top twenty-five knots in the afternoon. Another reason to get an early start.

At five a.m. when I woke, the breeze had already started in spite of the dense fog. By six a.m. I paddled away from my little turnout and into a dark gray void that slowly lightened as the sun rose behind hills I couldn't see. The wind in my face kept me chilled in spite of my constant effort, but at least the current was with me for a while. Three hours later, the mouth of Tomales opened to larger swells and thicker fog. Eighteen miles of exposed coast lay between me and the Pt. Reyes lighthouse. This was the go/no-go point. I could easily paddle back to my truck and call it a day, but going forward would commit me to the trip with no easy bailout option. I turned out to sea and pressed on.

The northwest side of Pt. Reyes is a crescent, and cutting a straight line from tip to tip saved me an hour of paddling compared to following the coast. Besides, to get close enough to see the shoreline in the heavy fog would risk getting caught inside the large breaking waves that pounded the rocks. Safer to navigate by compass and make a beeline, wind now at my side but remaining light.

The rhythm of long distance paddling settled in. My eyes glued to my deck compass, my body aware of every motion as it searched for maximum efficiency, my mind absorbing everything and nothing. Floating alone on the ocean brought peace, the awareness of being a tiny dot in the vastness of the sea, inconsequential and meaningless to the mass of water beneath. I felt in my place.

The sound of a whirring engine came out of the grayness and intruded on my tranquility. The noise grew as a small fishing boat formed out of the mist and turned to intercept my course. I figured they were worried about the poor little kayaker out on the big scary ocean, and I prepared to explain I knew what I was doing.

They pulled alongside, a pair of men in slickers aboard the skiff, and asked if I had a compass. I pointed to my bow and assured them I knew how to use it. But their concern wasn't for me—their GPS wasn't working, and they wanted to know where Bodega Bay was. Bodega lies ten miles north of Tomales, maybe fifteen miles from where we were, and across a stretch of open water. They were lost in the fog and wanted to get back home.

I looked at my chart and figured I could approximate a bearing to Bodega, but they wouldn't be able to follow it. I pointed toward shore, back the way I had come, and told them to follow it until they hit land.

"Veer left, keep the mainland on your right, and eventually you'll reach Bodega."

With many thanks they headed on their way, and I resumed my journey, more concerned for their well-being than my own. You never know who's going to need help on the ocean.

Mindless hours of paddling followed, with nothing but water and fog. The kind of slog that bores most paddlers but always energizes me. It reminded me of my early days, paddling out to the Channel Islands, in the middle of nowhere with no destination in sight. Life becomes very simple: trust your body and trust your course, one blade at a time, stay true. As if in reward for my diligence, the fog lifted to reveal the lighthouse when I reached the tip of land right on course and sooner than expected. The ocean turned blue like the sky, and the sun gleamed off the glass beacon high upon the cliff. I appreciated the view but knew sunshine brings with it a less pleasant friend.

The wind picked up immediately; strong gusts forced me toward the rocks. I paddled hard to pass the point until I was able to turn and head downwind, a short leg before I could tuck behind the point and make my way to the beach where my bike waited. Even heading downwind became a challenge as the wind howled with a sudden ferocity. Whitecaps sprouted all around and each gust threatened to rip my paddle from my hands. I surfed the waves forward, my paddle only needed to steer. A wild ride that lasted all too briefly as I turned once more to cross the wind and enter Drake's Bay and the home stretch.

I had assumed the large land mass would shield me from the northwest winds, but the opposite happened. The winds funneled over a depression in the ridge and accelerated down to slam into the water. If the steady wind was twenty-five knots, the wind across the bay was thirty-five and the gusts stronger. I'd been awake since five, paddled for eight hours, and covered thirty miles. The force of nature stopped me dead in my tracks and I swerved to the nearest beach for a break.

I hauled my boat onto the sand and considered sitting on a nearby log to eat some food, but instead hid behind a boulder that blocked the wind. The sun fed me energy as I filled my belly with protein bars and water. Closing my eyes for a few minutes restored my calm. The only way out was forward. I bounded up and shook my legs before cramming myself into the boat for one last effort. As I slid back into the water the log lifted its head and regarded me with indifference—a giant elephant seal soaking in the sun twenty feet away. I felt a kinship with the creature although he would have no trouble crossing the turbulent water. He was large and powerful, completely at home in the water and a natural part the world around him. Something to emulate.

Instead of taking a straight line, this time I hugged the shore, hoping for slightly less wind and more stopping spots if necessary. Head down, body fully engaged, I crossed the bay with a smile on my face and pain in my shoulders. This was preparation, training for my expedition, and I knew I would succeed.

The wind cut my pace half, and it took over an hour to cover the last couple miles. I reached Drake's beach utterly exhausted and totally exhilarated. I threw on extra layers to keep warm as I stowed my kayak gear and unlocked my bike. The fun wasn't over.

The bike ride started with a climb from the beach to the road at the top of the ridge. Stiff legs, tired from bracing and pumping while paddling, complained right away. In my lowest gear I crept up the hill, eventually dismounting to walk the final hundred yards. It took another gut check to remount and continue on.

The road along the ridge was winding and steep, dropping down for sharp curves at high speed and up hills that slowed me to a crawl. It was the hardest part of the day and by far the scariest. Each gust slid me several feet across the narrow road. I had to stay in the middle to keep from being blown into the ditch. Cars lined up angrily behind me and passed like rockets when I gave them a chance, creating more turbulence and making me wobble like a drunken fool. My muscles shuddered and at times I couldn't tell if the bike was shaking me or if I was shaking it. Part of me enjoyed the challenge, but in my weakened state my mind hung on for survival. One final, long downhill stretch brought me back to the water and my truck. My hands cramped squeezing the brakes, bringing me to a screeching halt next my trusty vehicle. I threw the bike in the back and slumped into the driver's seat.

But the trial wasn't over. When I returned to the beach to load my kayak the winds had increased. My first attempt at lifting my boat turned it into a sail and carried me across the sand to a hard landing. I dragged the boat over to the truck and carefully evaluated the loading procedure. If I sat it on the rack and let go for a moment it would fly off, smashing on the hard blacktop and ruining my expedition before it started. I reversed my truck and used the upright bars for my whitewater boats to hold the kayak. Never letting go, I tied down the front and swung the rear into the cradles, tying it down before undoing the front, sliding it over, and tying it back up. A normally five-minute operation, something that would have been easy with a companion or two, took half an hour of planning and deliberate action. In the end the boat was tied down securely and I headed home.

As physically tired as I was, the two-hour drive home didn't bother me. I was too excited and happy to be drowsy. This was the joy of paddling I remembered, hard work and challenge, uncertain outcome, but not death-defying. I earned the view of the lighthouse through my effort and skills, and made it across the bay on strength of will. And no one else had to put themselves at risk or even worry over me. I was ready for more.

Chapter 17

HAIDA GWAII

The inception of my British Columbia (B.C.) expedition came many years earlier in an off-hand conversation with Pedro. While paddling the Channel Islands, he talked about his dream trip, the Queen Charlotte Islands off the coast of northern B.C.—now known by the native name of Haida Gwaii (Islands of the People). So remote it takes two days to get there by plane and ferry, a wonderland of unspoiled old growth forest and hot springs, with a World Heritage Site containing the last of the Haida totem poles in their natural location. He never had the time to make the trip, but I did now.

I didn't invite Pedro on the trip. I didn't invite anyone. Aside from the reality that few people could run off for six weeks to go padding, I wanted the time by myself, to go where I pleased, change plans on a whim, and push myself without worrying about anyone else. My test run at Pt. Reyes confirmed I still had the ability to paddle long miles, navigate by compass, handle rough water, and generally do the solo thing.

And I wasn't just going to visit Haida Gwaii. I planned to circumnavigate the southern island, Moresby, which contains a national park and the most dramatic coastline, a trip of three hundred miles including a remote stretch on the exposed west coast known for brutal weather. Not for your average paddler, this was my dream expedition, and I didn't want to share it.

I made my way to B.C. through the San Juan Islands off the coast of Washington State, spending a few days at some friends' summer cabin in the area. I paddled long days for more training, weaving around the small islands, riding the currents, and gorging on local Rainier cherries bought from roadside stands on the way to launch. Each night I relaxed by reviewing charts of Haida Gwaii and programming camp sites into my GPS.

Before catching the short ferry to Vancouver Island and into Canada, I stopped off on Orcas Island to visit a kayak shop whose owner, Leon, had circumnavigated Moresby Island a few years before. He pointed out a few spots where currents could be tricky or waves a little challenging, but mostly spent his time highlighting the places not to miss on the rarely kayaked west coast. I took the hint of jealousy in his voice as a good sign.

More excited than ever, I hit Canadian soil and drove straight to Tofino, a popular destination for kayakers on the southwest side of Vancouver Island. A four-day trip out and back would serve as a shake-out paddle, testing out my camping gear and packing system. It's not that hard to fit everything into a seventeen foot sea kayak with the carrying capacity of two large backpacks, but weight distribution can greatly affect the kayak's performance, and organization is key to making sure important safety equipment—VHF radio, satellite tracking device, flares, and rescue equipment—is at hand when you need it.

As I packed on the beach to launch, a group of four middle-aged ladies landed, finishing their own three-day tour. They hadn't gone far, camping at the nearest island and covering a third of the distance I planned, but they beamed over the beauty of the scenery and named the many birds they saw. They were from South Carolina, the trip an annual tradition for them, a chance to get away from their husbands and reconnect with dear friends. They wished me good luck and waved me off. Part of the beauty of the sport is its accessibility to such a wide range of people with vastly different goals.

I headed north on the inside route, protected from winds and waves. A record heat spell made the paddling uncomfortable, reminiscent of southern California and not the B.C. chill I had prepared for. I peeled off layers at lunch, stowing my drysuit in a hatch. If I did go in the water I'd get cold all too quickly, but heat stroke was a more likely danger. A little slice of sand late in the day made for a private camp. I pitched my little tent but ended up sleeping under the stars, more than warm enough in my down sleeping bag. Alone in the wilderness, the adventure had begun.

The next day I covered twenty easy miles to land a short way from Hot Springs Cove, a popular destination visited by tour boats out of Tofino. After dinner, I paddled over to the cove, landing one beach down. A short hike brought me to the springs, a small trickle of water that gathered in natural pools of rock as it flowed into the sea. I had the place to myself and soaked in the lowest pool, the waves occasionally crashing over and inundating it with cold sea water before the steaming spring water forced it out and returned the warmth. Waves of hot and cold relaxed my body, making it hard to leave in time to reach my camp by sunset.

But eventually I did return to my site under a vermilion sky so beautiful I sat in my boat long after landing to watch the colors fade into blackness. I slept deep and hard but woke early to get in another soak before heading back toward Tofino.

The first trip in the books, everything working correctly, placement and choice of gear set, I moved north for a more ambitious excursion. On the way, I stopped for a short paddle in Johnstone Strait between Vancouver Island and the mainland, the most likely place to spot Orcas. I'd paddled next to dolphins, watched whales from my kayak, but had never seen an Orca outside Sea World. Launching from Telegraph Cove took me quickly into the Strait, and I followed the nearest whale watching boat, figuring their height would give them an advantage in spotting the black fins against the dark water. Sure enough, within an hour we found a pod and moved to parallel their course, a fishing trawler and sailboat joining the pursuit. At one point the whales turned and came within fifty yards, blowing loudly when they broke the surface. They moved with such grace and fluidity in the water, but they also dwarfed my kayak and left me feeling small and vulnerable. I was glad for the company watching them and paddled back to shore with another dream moment checked off my life list.

I crossed back over to the west side of the island for my next goal, a weeklong paddle around Brooks Peninsula and back. But the drive to the launch passed through heavy smoke, a wildfire burning somewhere in the area. It came from the north, but I couldn't tell the extent of the fire or what direction it headed. A family filled the informal campground at the end of the road, and they knew little more of the fire but planned to evacuate the next day just to be safe. I stayed the night, sleeping fitfully, worried about leaving my truck behind for a week while paddling in the direction of the fire. I'd be safe enough on the water, but if I came back to a burned out vehicle or a road blocked by fallen trees, I risked missing my ferry to Haida Gwaii. I couldn't take that chance and woke early to head back across the island to clean air and plan B.

I drove to Port Hardy, the departure town for the ferry. If I left from here, all I had to do was make it back in time for the ferry. No worries about fires or road closures or vehicle problems. I hadn't planned any paddling here, I didn't have any charts and neither did the local store, but I did have a guidebook that showed camping spots and a GPS loaded with a general map. Not the thorough preparation I liked to have for such a trip, but sometimes you make do with what you've got.

Port Hardy is on the inside of Vancouver Island and I paddled out and around Cape Scott on the northwest tip, hoping to find rougher waters and fewer people. The weather stayed mild and I shared most beaches with backpackers hiking the northern coastal trail though everyone seemed keen on their own privacy and a friendly wave from a distance was enough communication between groups. The few kayakers I spotted on the water followed the same example and I was left alone. Well, not exactly alone.

Every single day of the trip I paddled with whales, normally humpbacks popping up within spitting distance, the foul odor of their breath carrying across the water to alert me of their presence in case the throngs of circling birds or explosive spouts weren't enough. Steller sea lions, sea otters, and countless birds made guest appearances while a docile black bear shared my rocky campsite one evening. The highlight was paddling miles off Cape Scott to check out some offshore islands when a pod of Orcas crossed my path. The fog blanketed everything, hiding the land and muting the ocean, just me and these magnificent creatures intersecting in the middle of nowhere. I stopped to pull out my camera as the whales dove and disappeared. A minute passed, an eerie silence hanging in the air with a sense of anticipation, and then the entire pod surfaced at once, twenty yards away and headed straight for me. The camera couldn't focus on the all-too-close behemoths before they sunk into the depths, leaving a much starker silence and anticipation turned to fear. This was as alone on the ocean as it gets, and I didn't breathe until they did, coming up on my other side and swimming away. They had checked me out and left me unmolested. A good omen, and I waited for my pulse to calm like the water as I watched them fade into the distance.

The return to Port Hardy had more whales and birds, but nothing so dramatic as that pod of Orcas. I covered one hundred thirty-five files in seven days no problem, navigating off a guidebook and guessing at currents. No rough water but some good mental fortitude training. Time for Haida Gwaii.

⚬⟋⟍⚬

I left my truck at the ferry terminal and rolled my kayak onboard using collapsible wheels, everything loaded for two and a half weeks of self-sufficiency. I placed it in the kayak parking area—how cool is it that B.C. ferries have a designated area for kayaks! Over the next fourteen hours we made our way up the Inside Passage, a protected route between mountains on the mainland and a series of islands offshore.

The observation deck had comfy chairs to watch the green forest and cascading falls slide past. It was my birthday, and I treated myself to a huge chunk of chocolate cake from the cafeteria, a private celebration in the midst of families on vacation and college kids off to hike the wilderness. I was the only kayaker on board and certain no one planned a trip like mine.

We arrived in Prince Rupert after sunset, the six-hour ferry out to Haida Gwaii leaving early the next morning. I had hoped to sleep on a bench in the ferry building, but numerous signs made it clear that wasn't allowed. A campground sat a half mile toward town, and after everyone else cleared out, I rolled my kayak down the dark street. Loaded with gear and provisions, my kayak weighed a hundred and fifty pounds. It was a heavy load even with the wheels to help. I made it out of the parking lot and around the corner before deciding a half mile was too far this late at night, and much too far to repeat early the next morning. I noticed a side trail into the woods and followed it into darkness. A small clearing served my purpose and I slept wrapped in a tarp against the damp air, lying on wet grass next to my boat and hoping the morning would come soon.

I awoke at sunrise and returned to the terminal, the ferry right on time and the personnel again used to kayaks, blocking my wheels and tying it off so it wouldn't slide or roll in the waves. The trip out to Haida Gwaii leaves the safety of the barrier islands and crosses a hundred miles of open ocean. There's nothing protected about it.

The large ship docked at a quaint pier a mile from the tourist town of Queen Charlotte to the west and an equal distance from the working town of Skidegate to the east. Around the corner lay the Haida Heritage Centre where I needed to pick up my permit and attend a backcountry orientation before embarking on my trip. It was closed for the day and I paddled to a nearby island to camp, ready to be in the wilderness. A warm evening and glorious sunset made me optimistic for what was to come.

The orientation didn't start until eleven, so I spent the morning exploring the beautiful new museum at the Centre, complete with half a dozen giant totems out front. The Haida people carved large cedar trees into a series of animals to honor a person's life or death, raising them to mark a village site or individual homes. Once common across the islands, few old totems remain standing, and the museum featured several new poles by native craftsmen. From delicate argillite carvings, to intricate woven blankets, to giant dugout canoes, the artwork of the people highlighted the natural beauty of their land. I felt honored to take in this heritage before heading out to see the source for myself.

After the orientation and lunch, I launched from the shore at the Centre and paddled west for a counter-clockwise circumnavigation of Moresby Island. Nervous energy and excitement urged me to paddle hard, but significant currents and strong headwinds convinced me to stop early in the day. A narrow channel runs between Moresby and Graham Island to the north, a full day's paddle to reach the west coast. No point in fighting against the elements with so far to go.

An early start the next morning brought me to the end of the channel and the open ocean by midafternoon. Again I chose to stop instead of pressing on into more rugged waters. The early break allowed me to set up camp, have a nice dinner, and paddle across to Graham Island to search for the lost town of Cha'atl, mentioned in my guidebook as one of the few sites with old totems still standing.

I landed at the obvious little cove and headed into the woods. The light filtered through the tall canopy, a warm glow illuminating the many shades of green, from the lush moss, to the dark ferns, to the dried out leaves. No trails existed and nothing remained of a once prominent village. Abandoned a hundred years ago, the forest swallowed it up as if it never was. The only evidence of its existence a lone totem that stood surrounded by younger trees.

The pole had cracked in half and the carvings were faded by time. What had once been a grand marker was now hard to distinguish from the background. But it still held beauty, weathered and tilted like an old man barely able to stand, holding far more meaning the brightly painted poles of the Heritage Centre. This was the real Haida Gwaii.

The next day took me out to the coast amid ten-foot seas and strong winds. Comfortable in my boat, but worried about rogue waves, I stayed well offshore as I turned left and headed south. A line of white to my right signified a boomer, a large breaking wave with enough energy to smash my boat, and I veered farther out. Sometimes it's fun to follow the coast closely and explore the intricate features of the steep rock face, but sometimes caution trumps fun.

Shortly after my decision to stay in deep water I was greeted by a Minke whale, a smaller species than most whales but still large and powerful in the water. She circled me for ten minutes, clearly investigating this strange creature invading her environment, one that splashed the water to move along the surface. It felt like she said hello and goodbye with a raised tail fluke and deep dive. I stopped on the southern side of a large bay after a good day's paddle. So far so good.

But the forecast called for strong southwesterly winds and heavy rain the following day. Eager as I was to complete this exposed stretch of coast, I had built in some bad weather days to avoid risky decisions, knowing that the most dangerous point lay near the southern tip. I hated to use them up so early, but dawn brought miserable conditions and I stayed in my tent, occasionally poking my head out to confirm it still sucked. It always did, and I burned my way through the one book I brought with me, unable to walk more than ten feet into the dense forest that surrounded my little beach. Sometimes nature is boring.

Several fishing boats shattered my illusion of remoteness when they turned up mid-day, trolling just off my beach. The west coast of Moresby is lined with natural harbors cutting into the steep shoreline, and in a particularly large inlet just to the south lay a fishing camp, a floating village where scores of fisherman tied up for the night and spread out to ply the coast during the day. A loophole around the moratorium on building in this pristine wilderness, the water not as protected as the land. I suffered a day of engine noise and unfriendly stares.

When the winds let up the next morning, I hurried on my way and put as much distance between me and them as possible.

The fog rolled in by the time I approached my evening destination, obscuring the coastline and making it impossible to find the opening in the cliffs I wanted. To approach close enough to make out the shore would put me inside the surf zone and breaking waves. After ten hours on the water and unable to find my spot, I resorted to turning on my GPS and trusting it to guide me in through the waves. My preparation paid off, and I eased into the protected inlet for the night. Halfway down the west coast with good weather predicted ahead. A little farther and still good.

After a peaceful night, I launched in light rain and in a few hours reached Puffin Cove, crowded with its namesake birds and one of the wonders Leon had told me not to miss. Hidden away behind a rocky point of land is a narrow slot, no more than twenty feet wide, which opens up into a round bay of clear, calm water. An old cabin sits nestled in the trees, perched over a white sand beach like a guardian angel. Long abandoned, it once was home to a couple who fled the mainland and lived off the bounty of the land and kindness of passing strangers.

I took pictures but continued on my way, preoccupied with tomorrow's paddle and rounding McClean-Fraser Point, a treacherous bit of land infamous for strong currents and unpredictable weather. My guide book talked of calm days turning suddenly violent and blustery at the point, even under the best of conditions. It was the crux of my trip and I wanted to put it behind me as soon as possible.

I stopped at the last cove north of the point with the sun breaking through the clouds for the first time in days. I hung my clothes to dry and made camp, unable to relax. No current predictions exist for the point, but I knew my best chance to avoid currents was to pass at low tide early the next day. The forecast called for increasing winds throughout the day and the rest of the week. I needed to get past the point early, and I was too far away to do it. In a controlled frenzy, I ate a quick dinner and re-packed my boat to head further down the coast with only a couple hours of sunlight left, certain I'd find someplace to spend the night. I really didn't have a choice.

The clouds came back in as the sun dipped toward the horizon. The coast was barren and rocky. Time was running out when I found protection from the swells behind a finger of rocks where a small stream entered the ocean. But there was no beach, no flat area to land or set up camp. Nothing but a pile of boulders and rising tide.

With no other choice, I hopped out of my boat into chest-deep water, my drysuit holding out the water but not the cold. I walked my boat in and pulled it over rocks, the crunch of fiberglass on barnacles worse than fingernails on a chalkboard. Scratches didn't worry me, but if I cracked the hull and the boat starting leaking I could be delayed for days performing repairs. Unloading the boat reduced the weight, but I still had to pull it up ten vertical feet to get above the high water mark—tidal exchanges in the area frequently topped seventeen feet and it was hours before the water would stop rising. I moved with deliberate care, each step tested and solid before pulling the kayak a little higher, daylight gone and working by headlamp.

With my kayak secure on a high shelf, I unrolled my tent on a small patch of grass half as wide as necessary, with a three-foot drop on either side. I tied it to a stunted tree and tossed in all my gear as the raindrops fell again. Midnight came and went before I crawled into my sleeping bag, and I got little rest before my alarm beeped at four a.m. to reverse the process and break camp.

In the cold gray of pre-dawn, I slid my boat back down the rocks, getting it close to the water's edge. I packed up my tent and made several trips to stack my gear on a rock near my boat, eating a cold breakfast of granola bars in the process. When the sky lightened enough to put away my headlamp, I climbed into my drysuit and packed the boat, floating it on the water before loading the final heavy items. I waded out clear of the rocks and hopped onto the back deck, sliding my feet into the cockpit and shimmying forward into the seat before sealing my sprayskirt. Shivering, groggy, and apprehensive, I paddled hard to warm up and burn off nervous energy.

The rain came down in spits and spurts, the wind building behind me. I hit McClean-Fraser Point at low tide with no noticeable current but erratic winds and breaking waves. I rode the chaos for fifteen minutes before everything settled: the air, the water, and my nerves. Another two hours brought me to the southern point of Moresby and I turned the corner and headed in. The west coast behind me, I found the nearest beach and took a long nap still in my paddling clothes. It was all downhill from here.

Having completed the difficult section, my outlook changed dramatically. I looked at the trip as already over and a success, with the remaining paddling and trials mere formalities. I fell out of the moment and started thinking about what came next. What was my life after the paddling was done?

I still had great days and special moments: a private tour of Ninstints, a World Heritage Site; cruising through Burnaby Narrows teeming with underwater sea life and a bear following along on shore; storms and winds and a final day of sunshine to finish off. But nothing challenged me, nothing excited me. It all felt too easy, too transitory.

At the end of every day I was alone, with no one to share what I saw, no one to appreciate where I'd been. My accomplishment held little meaning of its own—this wasn't a race; I couldn't win. While I had enjoyed myself in the moment, I hadn't gotten anywhere, ending in the same place I began. I needed something more than paddling in my life.

The long road home gave me time to realize my life was already filled with something special: people. People who let me use their cabin for as long as I wanted, friends who'd do anything to help me on the river, strangers who passed along their experiences for my benefit. Through kayaking I had met wonderful people of all stripes and sizes, old and young, hardcore and soft. Maybe I wasn't a loner, not cut out for solo missions. Maybe I needed to focus less on the paddling and more on the company. Kayaking had opened my eyes, but it was time to see life through the filter of friendship.

A dolphin says hello during a crossing

Chapter 18

EXPEDITION IN THE BACK YARD

Back home after B.C., I embraced the paddling community. I returned to teaching for the company that laid me off, paddled with my local club on calm lakes, with less experienced friends on class III whitewater, and started a blog that allowed me share my thoughts and feelings on the sport. No longer worried about accomplishments, kayaking became a means to an end and not an end in itself; a medium to reach other people and enjoy beautiful places. Part of me still wanted to push myself, to use my skill and experience to do something cool. But not alone this time.

There was no one I'd rather share an adventure with than Pedro, the person responsible for introducing me to kayaking in the first place. He still lived in Los Angeles, and we hadn't seen each other in years, but we got back in touch and resumed our easy friendship. I said it was finally time for us to complete the Channel Islands, and Pedro was in.

It wasn't really as simple as that. Pedro was married with a couple young kids; paddling didn't really fit into his busy life. He needed to get into shape and secure vacation time at work and support from his family. I needed to coordinate my schedule and work out the logistics—it would take a lot of logistics.

There are eight Channel Islands that stretch from Santa Barbara to San Diego: five northern islands that make up a National Park, Catalina just south of Los Angeles, and two remote islands owned by the military and often used for live bombing practice. Pedro and I had been to the first six, and our friend Duane had paddled to San Clemente, one of the military islands. But no one had paddled to San Nicholas, the other military island. Landing was not allowed, but certain sections of water were open to private boaters, making it possible to kayak close enough to touch the shore. Since those two are the farthest out, each require a round trip of seventy to eighty miles to reach them and return to an island where you can actually get out of your kayak again. That's more than twenty-four hours of non-stop paddling. To visit all eight islands in one trip would take two weeks, covering almost 500 miles, paddling on average 45 miles a day. Pedro wasn't the only one who needed to improve his fitness for the trip.

As our plans became more concrete our excitement grew, and I wanted to share the fun with the few friends I thought would be capable of such a trip. We invited Duane to join us without a second thought. Both Pedro and I had done several trips with Duane, including a crossing to Santa Barbara Island years before that covered a hundred miles in forty-eight hours. Not only could he handle the distance, he probably had more experience paddling the Channel Islands than anyone alive. And he's full of entertaining stories and good cheer—during that Santa Barbara trip Pedro got seasick, and Duane sang old sailor tunes to take his mind off the misery. What more could you ask for in a companion? Unfortunately, Duane decided his days of long distance paddling were done. He wished us well but passed on the trip.

I also invited a northern California friend, Sean, though it wasn't as simple a decision. He didn't know Pedro and had never paddled the Channel Islands. We worked together but lived hours apart and had never paddled together for fun. With a background in kayak racing, and major expeditions under his belt that dwarfed anything I had done, Sean easily had the skills and endurance necessary for the trip. But you never really know how you'll get along with someone when you're out in the wild and life gets difficult. It was a bit of a gamble, but my new attitude was all about inclusion—something I learned from Alex on the river. The more the merrier.

Sean jumped at the chance, the trip on his personal radar already. No one had ever paddled to all eight of the islands, and doing something for the first time was a big draw. Our team of three seemed the perfect crew. We fixed a date in the early fall, when the weather would be most favorable, and prepared. I arranged to borrow a longer, faster boat from a friend, Sean ordered a custom boat from one of his sponsors, Pedro dusted off his kayak, and we all packed on the miles in separate training.

As the launch date approached, I drove down to L.A. to pick up my loaner kayak for the trip and spend the day packing equipment with Pedro. Two weeks' worth of food, water for five days (we'd only be able to refill on a couple of the islands), paddling equipment, camping equipment, charts, cameras, and plenty of sunscreen—no drysuit needed for paddling in these waters. We packed everything into the boats to make sure it fit, then unpacked and loaded it all into the car for the ride north. We met Sean in Santa Barbara, and a local paddler kindly shuttled us to the campground, the very same one where my first Channel Islands expedition began many years before.

The last time we launched in the dark, afraid to get caught by the winds and unsure of how long the twenty-six mile crossing would take us. This time we waited for the dawn, confident in our ability to handle the distance and a gentle forecast on our side. The blue sky and clear air gave perfect visibility, the oil derrick our first marker and the island visible not long after that. We cruised along, Pedro and I reminiscing about the past and Sean soaking in stories of the islands. Pods of dolphins danced around us and eight hours flew by. We landed on San Miguel early in the afternoon, riding two-foot waves onto the soft sand as a fog bank enveloped the back of the island. Easy peasy.

We hiked up the steep hill to the campground and found it empty. After pitching tents, we napped in the sunshine until the sea fog spread to swallow the sun, and the air grew moist and chill. Sitting around a wooden table, cooking dinner over tiny camp stoves, we discussed the day.

Sean worried we took too long in the crossing, our speed not fast enough for the legs ahead. Pedro's back bothered him and he wasn't sure if he could go faster. I knew we were a little slow, but it often takes a few days to get into the rhythm on a big trip. The next day's paddle to Santa Rosa Island was a little shorter, so hopefully it would go faster and give us plenty of time to rest.

Still confident, we chose to take the scenic route to Santa Rosa by paddling around the southern tip of San Miguel, once again visiting the rookery at Pt. Bennett. Sean wanted to see the place for himself and it didn't disappoint, teeming with elephant seals and sea lions, and the sad but magnificent body of a blue whale washed up on shore. But our pace was even slower than the previous day. Pedro hurt.

Instead of continuing to follow the shore, we cut straight across to the southern point of Santa Rosa Island, shaving a few miles off the route. We camped on the same beach we had used on that first trip, the new expedition copying the details of the old. More concerns were expressed and we all agreed to get an earlier start the next day, the crossing to Santa Cruz Island the longest distance yet but still far shorter than what lay ahead. We shared dinner and smiles, enjoyed the isolated beach, and talked about life and paddling.

Tension lurked underneath it all. Sean worried about Pedro, an unknown paddler to him whose injury put our goal in jeopardy. Pedro was clearly upset with himself and in a lot of pain. I tried to captain the ship and hope for the best.

We launched in the dark, a cold wave to the face a better wake-up than all the coffee in the world. Pedro and I headed away from shore and straight toward the bottom of Santa Cruz, saving us miles but exposing us to any wind that might arise. Our experience told us that calm mornings usually lasted until midday. This approach worked the day before as well as the first time we had made this very crossing. Sean hung to the shore, his greater speed making up for the longer distance. It all went fine for the first few hours, but by ten a.m. the west wind arrived and funneled between the gap in the islands, creating a crosswind for us to fight and slowing our forward progress. Caught in no man's land, Pedro and I pushed on, me out in front hoping to spur him to a little more speed.

Sean's route exposed him to the wind for a briefer period, but he changed his course and paddled over to me. Visibly upset, he complained about my choice of route and questioned how I could make such a foolish decision. I explained my reasoning but a rough ocean isn't the place for a measured discussion. Besides, there was nothing to do at this point besides continuing on. Sean headed back into shore, easily pulling away and giving us space. We kept in sight but separate until Pedro and I eventually made it back near shore and out of the wind. There was nothing more to say, and we all stayed together for the rest of the trip.

Rounding the eastern tip of the island we faced even stronger headwinds for the last few miles to camp. It was all Pedro could do to make headway. We were all fatigued when we landed late in the day, the campground already in shade from the fading sun. With everyone deep in their own thoughts, we agreed to take a rest day tomorrow. We turned in as darkness fell.

In spite of our slow pace, I had enjoyed the paddling, happy to be back in what felt like home with good company. Pedro never let his agony interfere with his positive attitude, and Sean did everything he could to help. Everyone was supportive and understanding, but it was my trip and success looked doubtful. I couldn't will us to victory and couldn't let go of the responsibility. I slept little that night.

A leisurely morning and light hiking delayed talk of paddling and gave us time for more reflection. When we sat down in the afternoon to make plans, it was a meeting of like-minded individuals determined to find the best solution for everyone. Pedro bowed out, willing to paddle to the mainland by himself. He didn't want to slow us down any longer. Sean wanted to continue, still strong and optimistic. I stood on the fence and teetered.

I felt strong and capable though unsure if I had the speed Sean possessed. If I continued with him, I might be the one holding him back. I worried more about Pedro paddling alone while injured than Sean making large crossings on his own—he had done longer crossings in harder conditions and could take care of himself. In the end, I used safety as a convenient excuse to avoid failure and chose to accompany Pedro. Everyone seemed happy with the choices given the circumstances we faced. Pedro and I shared all our local knowledge, as well as a few bits of gear, in the hopes that it would help Sean accomplish the goal. If we couldn't be the first to paddle to all eight Channel Islands, we wanted it to be our friend.

We all launched early the next morning but said our goodbyes before Sean bolted off, a forty mile day to reach Santa Barbara Island in front of him. Pedro and I paddled over to Anacapa, not the shortest distance home, but we both wanted to recreate the whole route from our first expedition. No longer worried about speed, content in our decision to bail out, we soaked in sun and contentment as the wind blew at our backs and carried us across to the mainland.

I enjoyed that last day of paddling the most. The company had been stellar the whole time, the scenery and remoteness better before, the challenge and excitement greater at the beginning, but the drive to reach a goal had taken away some of the pleasure. That drive can be a good thing, urging you to greater heights and personal accomplishments. But a focus on results undercuts the joy of the journey itself. An adventure is an outing where the outcome is uncertain. If you accept that, then the one certainty is enjoyment. I felt closer to understanding my life through kayaking, but the perfect balance still eluded me.

Pedro's wife and the kids picked us up when we landed, and I observed a joy beyond paddling when his girls jumped out of the car and swarmed him with hugs and questions. It put kayaking in its place. Our adventure was a little side trip that only made him appreciate the important things all the more. He hadn't failed out there any more than I had the first time he tried to teach me how to catch a wave off Catalina. He was succeeding in life, and I envied the many adventures he had in front of him.

Sean made it to Santa Barbara Island and started the next day for San Nicholas, the most remote of the planned trip. The weather turned against him and he wisely retreated, crossing over to Catalina and meeting a too-curious Blue Shark along the way. No harm to his boat, only his nerves, he made it safely to the mainland, having visited six of the Islands in one grand trip. If I had joined him it wouldn't have helped, and possibly hurt, so it all worked out for the best. No one reached the original objective, but everyone got something worthwhile out of the experience. I had a lot to think about.

Sheltering from the rain

Chapter 19

DESCENDING THE RUBICON

In In my quest to find the perfect paddling recipe, I stepped it back a notch. No large expeditions, no exploratory missions, stick to familiar and fun, with people I knew and enjoyed. Keep it simple.

I had been reinstated as the program manager at my old company, working full time largely in the office. My career was in the same place it had been five years earlier, only with a lower salary. I knew I didn't want it to be my future, but I was as afraid to venture into the unknown at work as I was on the water. I was comfortable. I got by. Why risk it?

But the paddling gods knew how to tempt me. The river had more lessons to teach. The snowpack in California sat well above average for the first time in years, and the runoff promised an epic whitewater season. More water, more rivers, and everyone wanted in on the action. I took it easy and ticked off a couple new runs but nothing crazy. I met up with Alex to run a creek near Los Angeles that had long been on my list though it turned out easier and less picturesque than advertised. I ran some new class IV rivers with my local friend Matt, building my confidence back up. Then word spread that the Rubicon was going to run.

The Rubicon River comes off the back side of Lake Tahoe, only two hours from Sacramento, with easy road access, yet still passes through twenty miles of almost untouched wilderness—except where the famed jeep trail of the same name crosses its course. Reputed to have some of the best whitewater in a state full of world-renowned rivers, no one I knew had ever paddled it. That's because it's damned up and only runs when the reservoir at its head overflows during a big run-off. A once in a lifetime opportunity.

Everyone talked about getting on the Rubicon, but no one seemed sure what was a good flow level. The first people who rushed in reported low water and lots of willows clogging the river bed. The next group reported high flows that scared them off a mile into the run. I watched the levels and put out feelers to my friends—I only wanted to go in with people I trusted. A weekend passed with everyone still worried it was too high, but Monday saw flows drop and the window opened. Texts flew back and forth and a crew rallied.

But rallied at a kayaker pace, which means slow. Some folks had to work in the morning, Matt was in Oregon but driving back to make the trip, the rest of us had to pack food for an overnighter and organize the shuttle. We left my truck at the takeout expecting a group of four; by the time we all converged at the put-in late in the day, we numbered seven, the new additions strong paddlers and a benefit to the team. I knew them all, some better than others, and couldn't ask for a better gang to hit the Rubicon.

We launched into the unknown and immediately felt the power of the water. The gauge put the flow at eleven hundred cfs, but it felt stronger in the rocky channel. Without regular flushes to clear the river, willows grew thick in the eddies, making it near impossible to stop, especially with so large a group. Our best kayakers led the way, and we dropped into rapids en masse, trusting the person ahead to indicate dangers and hoping to react fast enough to avoid them. It was hard, technical whitewater, exhilarating and frightening. Moving in such a fashion, it was only a matter of time before someone ran into something unpleasant. I drew the short straw.

On one blind corner, I misread the line and got swallowed by an enormous hole, flipping me instantly as I tucked to survive the ride. Hoping for a pause to orientate myself, I got none. Bubbles of aerated water blurred my vision as the river tossed me end over end. My boat hit something hard and the force of the current ripped the paddle from my hands. Time to eject, but the water pinned me to the back of my boat, unable the reach the release tab to pull my sprayskirt. The beat down continued and my face brushed passed the hard object—a log pinned against the rocks. I muscled myself forward enough to yank my tab, straining my abdominal muscles in the process, and let the water suck me out of my kayak. I went down into darkness, praying for air soon. My wish granted, I popped up free of the hole and within an easy swim to shore where one of my buddies waited to help.

The others collected my gear and we regrouped and continued on our way. We only planned on one night out, meaning we needed to cover as much ground as possible before darkness to make the second day short enough to finish. More big holes followed, mostly avoided or kind enough to spit out the haggard boater. But not all—we stopped after yet another monster hydraulic forced one more swim in our group. Dusk descended as we chose a sandy beach to call home for the night.

We called it a successful day one, no injuries (other than my sore abs), no lost gear, plenty of wide eyes and oh-crap moments. A roaring campfire and warm California night made for a fine recovery, everyone happy with the adventure so far. After s'mores and cheap whiskey, everyone found a piece of sandy beach to throw down their sleeping pad. Camping in the open, along the river in a remote place, is one of the greatest rewards for paddling class V whitewater in the sunshine state.

The second day started slow, but at least we put on in the morning. We knew we had a big day to get out in time, and once on the river we moved as fast as we could.

The river didn't cooperate. The rapids grew longer and harder, we had to get out to scout often, and most of our group walked around the hardest drops. Most rivers have difficult patches split up by easier sections where you can catch your breath; the Rubicon had hard parts separated by much harder spots, consistently as difficult as anything I'd ever done.

I paddled as well as I ever had, finding some ugly lines but always fighting my way through and out of danger. It was great to be on the edge of my comfort zone, totally focused and in the moment. The joy was short-lived.

Our group had a couple more swims, and we grew slower, more cautious. We still had a long ways to go when it started to sprinkle in the afternoon. Matt got pinned against a willow, trapped in his boat for a minute before he could release himself and swim to safety. It took longer to recover his boat. The clouds darkened the sky and our moods, rain falling steadily. Everyone was intent on getting out, a mindset driven by the scary paddling, dropping temperatures, and lack of camping gear. No one came prepared for a second night out, no one carried a tent or tarp—it never rains in June in California. Just like the Rubicon never has water in it. Exceptions can be a bitch.

After another scary swim we rafted up on shore to discuss our options. Matt was out of fun tickets, I was exhausted and not alone on that count, but Isaac, one of the strongest paddlers, insisted we continue. All peers makes for a great team, but sometimes it's hard to reach a decision without a captain. Realistically, I was one of the weakest in the party; I hadn't been paddling much hard whitewater and didn't have the experience of the others. But I knew how to make decisions. I looked at the faces in the circle, people I knew and cared about. The consensus was there, but no one wanted to say it. I shook my head gently at Isaac.

"We're done. No more paddling today. We need to find a campsite."

Everyone nodded, including Isaac, and people contributed to the plan.

"Let's keep going as long as the river is easy."

"Look for someplace sheltered from the rain, a cave or hollow tree."

"I've got extra food to share."

We floated around the corner and someone spotted a cave above a gravel bar. It wasn't large, barely big enough for all seven of us to huddle under its lip, but it felt like a miracle find in the cold rain. We gathered wood and Isaac started a roaring fire while everyone shared whatever food they had left. Puddles formed on the rock floor, and people lay on their overturned boats in a feeble attempt to stay dry. I volunteered to sleep outside, using an emergency blanket as a tarp and hoping my ancient waterproof sleeping bag still lived up to the claim. Cold, wet, hungry, and miserable, we turned in expecting the rain to stop at any moment. It didn't.

Utterly exhausted as I was, I didn't sleep that night. The wind tugged at my small blanket, water snuck past and soaked my bag. I held the thin Mylar over my face so at least my head would stay dry. I lay shivering, the drip drip of water a constant torture, and worried what the next day would bring. I rose at dawn, rain still falling gently and the fire now out, and stirred the others to begin our (hopefully) final day on the Rubicon. We roused the fire and chased away the chill from our bones, but it did nothing to banish the feeling of dread in the air.

We started without discussion, the simple plan of moving downstream as fast as possible unchanged. Not surprisingly, more people swam. I flipped in a class four rapid up against a wall and simply lacked the energy to roll. The continuous nature of the river meant I swam for a quarter mile, dropping into holes and going through waves, swallowing water and barely able to stay afloat. My friend Taylor caught up to me, and I hung onto to his stern for dear life, but there was nowhere to stop and get out. Willows filled every shallow, and swimming into them meant getting pinned and possibly drowning. More class V rapids lay ahead, and I needed to get out of the water now.

Passing a rock face, I grabbed a knob sticking out, trading my death-grip on the kayak for one on something stationary. It was all I could do hold on and not be swept downriver, but my friends on the opposite shore pointed downstream and then drew their fingers across their throats, the sign for deadly hazard. They pointed up and I started climbing.

Near vertical, the granite slab rose thirty feet before rounding into the trees. For someone with my climbing experience, it wasn't too difficult, but a slip would send me falling back into the river and toward the unseen danger below. I moved quickly, riding my adrenaline high and knowing the energy wouldn't last long, wedging my booties into tiny crevices and crimping my fingers to pull my body up. At the top I could see downstream, a couple of guys on shore with my boat above a large waterfall. The rock sloped more gently in their direction, and I pointed to the others to meet up there. All my gear had been rescued before the drop, and after a quick look we all walked around and put on below. No time for reflection, not even for fear. We had to keep moving.

More close calls led to a team meeting. We knew that a side stream entered the river near the end, with only one difficult rapid between it and the take-out. If we could reach that stream, we would know we were close to home. Isaac said it was time to stop scouting, that the difficult stuff was behind us, and we had to keep moving and trust the leaders to find the lines. I had no energy to speak or protest, couldn't even shake my head, but others did it for me. The crew was beat, physically and mentally, and we needed caution now more than ever. The only thing we agreed on was the need to keep moving.

Right after we started paddling again a horizon line stretched across the river, hiding a noisy rapid below and unknown danger. Isaac and Taylor charged in, but the rest of us held back. Unable to see the outcome, unwilling to follow, we got out to scout.

The dense forest made it hard to walk and impossible to see downstream. We carried our boats, expecting the worst and reasoning that an immediate portage would be quicker than a scout and eventual portage. Fifteen minutes of bushwhacking brought us to the hidden rapid, a ledge stretched across the entire river, creating an unavoidable reversal that would swallow our multicolored kayaks like Flintstone's vitamins.

The view flipped a switch in my mind. My brain had locked on paddling down the river, the only way out. Now I saw the truth: the rain-swollen river was a beast, no longer fit for kayaking. We later found that the flow rose to over four thousand cfs, way above a safe level. We needed to get out, but the river wasn't the only option. It wasn't even a realistic one.

Once again, the act of opening ourselves up to possibilities was immediately rewarded when one of the guys spotted a trail above us. Climbing up a short ways revealed a dirt road in surprisingly good condition. It climbed up the hillside, undoubtedly to the main road, and from there a short walk to my truck. A safe way out for us, but two of our seven were still on the river, somewhere below the rapid. We didn't even know if they made it through the hole okay. We called out, used our whistles, even tried to hike downstream as far as possible. With no sign or signal, no way to get down to them, not sure if they needed help or were fine, the only thing we could do was hike out, get to the take-out as fast as possible, and hope they made it down alive. They were the best kayakers in the group, truly world-class. If anyone could paddle a flooded class V river, they could.

The hike was surprisingly easy once we left our boats and gear behind. The road climbed steadily, reaching the paved shuttle road on a high ridge. The rain stopped and California sunshine returned. A pair volunteered to walk to the truck, getting lucky and hitching a ride with the first passing vehicle while the rest of us napped roadside.

My truck wasn't at the take-out but the confusion was quickly relieved when Isaac pulled up with Taylor, the pair having paddled out safely and made a quick run into town to call home and pass the word we were safe. They also brought back pizza and fried chicken. We drove down the dirt track to retrieve our boats, then up the river to the rest of the cars at the put-in. As simple as that, the ordeal was over, and everyone returned to their warm beds for a dry night's sleep.

The trip hung with me for a long time afterward. The Rubicon represented the best paddling of my life, charging down class V rapids, running blind drops and enjoying a gorgeous night under the stars. It also held memories of abject terror and a miserable night under an insufficient space blanket. We worked as a smooth unit at times, passing information up the line and using teamwork to ease portages, but the team broke down under pressure, with heated arguments and the eventual split of the group. The good and bad, I took it all and wouldn't trade it for anything less. Neither would I ever want to repeat it.

It's impossible to get the highs in life without risking the lows. Staying at home, being comfortable and safe would never satisfy me. I needed to push myself, to excel, in order to find happiness. There had to be a way to do that without putting my life on the line, physically and metaphorically. My search for balance continued.

Chapter 20

OFF THE COUCH

I knew my days as a program manager were numbered. I still loved the instruction, but the rest of the work simply didn't inspire me. When the owner of the shop approached me about buying him out, it didn't take a lot of thought to turn him down. Sure, owning a kayak business was a real future, but not one I wanted. It was a future of business decisions, managing staff and watching margins, spreadsheets and office time. I knew I had the skills, and while I'm sure it would have been a lot of hard work and years of effort, I felt certain the outcome would be fine. I wanted something new. I wanted a career that gave me what paddling did: excitement, challenge, fulfillment, and pleasure.

My blog had renewed a long-dormant passion for writing, spurring me to dabble in fiction and dream of completing a novel. Half the fun of kayak trips was writing them up afterward. I began to study the craft and explore what it would take to become an author. A new dream grew.

In the meantime, long hours at work kept me busy and writing sucked up my off days. Paddling fell on the list of priorities. I still wanted to kayak, still wanted to spend time with my friends, but didn't know how to fit it into the rest of my life. An invite from Sean to join a mini-expedition to explore the Lost Coast helped show me the way.

California has a long and beautiful coastline, followed diligently by Highway One for almost its entire length. One section of coast in northern California is too rugged, too steep and dangerous, to allow any road to share its space. The seventy-five-mile roadless stretch between Eureka and Fort Bragg is known as the Lost Coast. It's exposed and rocky, containing the westernmost point of the state where Cape Mendocino juts into the Pacific, and a kayaker's paradise—if you have the skills to handle it.

Sean invited two other instructors on the trip, bringing the total to four experienced rough-water paddlers. And while it would have been nice to have a flexible launch date and some buffer days built in for nice weather, we all had busy lives and other commitments. We squeezed in a four-day block on the calendar and scrutinized the forecast. With no flexibility, we would take what we got and make the best of it.

The goal for the trip wasn't simply to cover the distance. Sean's passion is playing in the rocks, exploring the nooks and crannies of a coastline up close and personal. To do that, we all chose shorter, plastic sea kayaks, not the long expedition boats like we used for the Channel Islands. The short length makes them more responsive and better at surfing and dodging rocks; the plastic makes them tough and better able to survive an impact when you're unsuccessful in your rock dodging. Both things also make the boats slower, with less room for storage. Covering the distance in such boats, playing along the way, in possibly rough conditions, wouldn't be easy, even under the best conditions.

At the time, the only paddling I did was for work. Beginner classes or lake tours—nothing that involved long, hard paddling and the training I could use. The whitewater season months earlier had toughened me up with strenuous days on the Rubicon and other rivers, but it's a completely different thing, wind sprints versus marathon running. Physically, I wasn't in shape for the Lost Coast, but I had skills and experience to draw on. Mentally, I was completely ready for it.

We met early on the first day at Sean's place in the Bay Area, loading four boats onto my truck as he followed along in his vehicle, dropping it off at the south end of the route for shuttle—this was definitely a one way trip. All four paddlers then loaded into my rig, and we circled inland on Highway One, eventually returning to the sea at a nondescript beach outside of the little town of Ferndale. The tide high, the surf moderate, we assessed the conditions and agreed a launch was feasible. By the time boats were loaded and we made it through the surf one at a time, it was six p.m. and only a couple hours of sunlight remained. A mile of paddling took us past the road's end and into the Lost Coast proper. Five more miles brought us to a protected beach and campsite for the night. A short start, but essential to get some distance in the books and shorten the next three days as much as possible.

The next morning dawned sunny and calm, a rarity on the northern coast. Sean and I packed up quickly, hoping to take advantage of the conditions and not expecting them to last. The other two were experienced paddlers but not used to long mileage expeditions. They took longer to break down tents and put away stoves, to fit everything into our over-stuffed boats and prepare to launch. It was okay; the weather held and we made good speed on the water.

I worked hard to keep up with the others, my boat feeling slow and heavy even though I knew their boats were no different. I figured I was more out of shape than I thought, but I gritted my teeth and focused on my touring technique, a different style than I used on the river—I needed to get every ounce of efficiency out of my effort. Midday we rounded Cape Mendocino, the water dotted with large rocks and conditions mellow enough for us to cruise between them, making our way to shore for a lunch break.

There I discovered my stern compartment completely filled with sea water, somehow my hatch hadn't sealed properly and I carried a couple hundred extra pounds with me as I paddled. No wonder I felt sluggish. Chagrined at my rookie mistake, I emptied out the boat and double-checked the hatch cover when we launched. Miraculously, I no longer had to work so hard to stay with the group.

We paddled late into the day, the scenery nice but the play potential limited. It takes a special kind of rock to be fun on the ocean. Caves and tunnels make things interesting, small rocks create pourovers—rocks you can paddle over when a wave covers it—and slots and channels provide an obstacle course to run. The rocks we had were large and widely spaced, with no features to create excitement. We expected things to get better the further south we went, so we pushed on.

Everyone was tired as we neared our goal for the night, a surfers' secret camp. Not much of a secret, a short bluff stuck out into the ocean and created a well-known but rarely visited surf break, with plenty of flat grass for camping. Sean was dying for some surf, but the rest of us just wanted rest. Even with my lighter boat, my forearm and wrist hurt from so much hard paddling in the morning. Now every stroke was accompanied by a stabbing pain. When we found the beach, and the surf was too small to play on, I happily landed and called it a day. Thirty-five miles in a loaded boat not meant for such distance was enough.

The next morning we got a quicker start, and I took time to loosen up my arm and pop back several Ibuprofens. It kept the pain away for the morning as we sailed down to Shelter Cove, still blessed with plentiful sun and light winds at our back. Around Shelter Cove, the only town on the Lost Coast, we found some rocks to play in. Directly under the city's bluff lay a small reef, the increasing swells breaking on the outside with outcroppings and slots on the inside. Sean and I rode the surging channels, carefully avoiding crashing waves and timing moves from one protected position to another. It was good to finally use our boats for the reason we brought them, but the extra effort overpowered the painkillers and a needed lunch break afforded me time to raid my medicine bag.

My arm hurt the rest of the day, but the pain was manageable and my mood lightened by the arches and tunnels we found at the base of the cliffs. We took turns paddling through cracks in the rock, sunlight streaming in behind and the ocean swell pushing us through. Sean found a tunnel with multiple entrances and large enough to fit all four of us at once. We floated in the dark, our laughter echoing off the walls along with the incoming waves. This is what we came for.

Our pace slowed but we never stopped, our play always leading us further south. We quickly explored the numerous rock towers sitting just outside our harbor for the night, but hunger and encroaching darkness sent us to shore. We made camp on the beach and climbed a ridge to watch the sun set, the pale disc dropping into dark water and diffusing an auburn glow through the sky. Pelicans streaked past the rocks as if highlighting where we should look for play in the morning. All pain forgotten, I stayed until darkness swallowed the last glow of light and a cool breeze stirred the air.

Our final day continued the streak of fine weather, and I stayed on the ridge to photograph the others playing among the rocks. My forearm stiffened overnight and it took more time and drugs to loosen it up. The others didn't play long, and I joined them on the water, twenty-five miles to cover with the wind against us now. We saw more rock gardens to explore but dallied in only a few, pressing on to complete the trip.

Nearing the end of the lost section of coast, where Highway One returns to follow the jagged shoreline, the winds picked up, slowing us to a snail's pace. This is where we paid for our choice in boats and rush to finish in four days. A wide, protected bay offered a moment's respite and we ducked in to land on the beach and gather our energy for one last push. Sean was as strong as ever, but his boat the slowest of the lot. My arm ached, but the pain now familiar and easy to block out. The other two were tuckered out and the beach offered an alternative.

People walked across the sand and their vehicle sat back from the shore—a road accessed the bay. If someone paddled on to retrieve Sean's truck, they could drive back and pick up the rest of the crew here. Sean was game—it was his truck and he had no problem fighting the wind and doing it alone if necessary. I chose to join him this time; I wanted to finish this trip properly. I had the skills and the strength, pain not an acceptable excuse to bow out.

The two of us hit the water and found the wind fiercer outside the bay. Half an hour of struggle made me question my choice. Sean slowly pulled away, and I thought about turning back, not wanting to slow him up. But I didn't. I could do this.

We passed a sharp point of land and the wind died dramatically. I caught up to Sean and without a word we cruised on side by side.

But the drama wasn't over. The wind gone, the fog came in, shrouding the shore in an impenetrable gray. The swells had grown steadily over the trip, our ability to choose only the most protected landings had saved us from dangerous surf zones the last few days. Now we had no choice in our destination; we had to land near our vehicle, but we couldn't even see the shore, much less a small silver truck in the colorless mist. The surf we could see broke far out, with powerful sets crashing ten feet high. Sean was literally a world champion surf kayaker, having won the title a year earlier in Santa Cruz. I trusted him to find the best route through the waves, but I didn't trust myself to handle what he was capable of.

We talked our thoughts out together, pointing out landmarks we saw and remembering the shape of the coast from when we dropped off the truck four days earlier. I voiced my concern about following him in and he accepted my worries and expressed confidence in us both. We joked that the beauty of landing in surf is even if you wipe out terribly the waves still deposit you on the beach. One way or the other, we would make it in.

The fog let up enough for us to recognize a strip of shore, and we both agreed our goal lay behind a field of rocks. If we made it through the hazard zone, quite likely the beach itself would be protected. Sean took point and I stayed close enough to watch him pick his way but far enough back to give him room if a wave caught us by surprise. A couple minutes of tense paddling saw us safely through, my faith in him and his in me justified. The sight of manageable four-foot waves on the beach brought out a smile. No problem; I had this.

After an easy landing we emptied the boats and schlepped the gear up the steep trail to the truck, coming back to carry the boats one at a time. We threw the wet stuff in the back and tied the kayaks on the roof, eager to get on the road and find our waiting buddies. Locating them wasn't as straightforward. The beach was on our map, but the road to it wasn't. After a few times up and down the stretch of road, we found a turnout to an open gate which lead in the right direction. Following it took us to our friends. We got luckier than we knew: the beach is private and the gate at the entrance normally locked. But the people walking the sand took pity on our tired companions and opened the gate, the one Sean and I passed blithely through. The kindness of strangers a common trait in such remote settings.

During the long drive up to retrieve my truck, and my longer drive home from there, I basked in the joy of success. It wasn't just that I had completed the paddle or been able to keep up with Sean, but the realization that this is what my paddling career had prepared me for. Kayaking wasn't the center of my life, but I still had a passion for it. My job consumed more time, my writing took up more thoughts, and my friendships were more valuable, but they all connected in paddling, and through years of training and dedication I had earned the ability to jump off the couch and complete a long, hard trip most kayakers only dream about. This is how kayaking fit into my future.

Gilbert dropping into Carson Falls

Chapter 21

PERFECTION

After the Lost Coast I poured myself into writing. I gave myself specific exercises, setting up a workout regimen similar to my polo training. I went further, from short stories to novellas, stretching my distance like I had on my first crossing to the Channel Islands. I struggled, I doubted myself. I knew my path held great risk and no assurance of success. But I stuck with it. All while running an ever-growing kayak program.

I knew I needed to commit to writing, but was afraid to leave a stable paycheck and the good life I had built in the paddling world. I hesitated.

As I pondered my future path, Gilbert sent a message from Kernville inviting me on an overnight trip down the Forks of the Kern over Memorial Day weekend. He was only inviting good friends and strong paddlers. Could I make it?

My job wouldn't allow it—holidays are big business in the kayak industry. I was scheduled to be in the store, selling things to people looking to put some recreation in their life. The dichotomy brought a clarity and realization. I gave my two weeks' notice and asked Gilbert when and where to meet. Time to peel out of the eddy and see what lay over the horizon line.

The trip shaped up better than I could have hoped: Matt carpooled with me from NorCal, coming to celebrate his birthday on the river; Alex drove up from Los Angeles with news of his upcoming move to the Bay Area; more old friends and a couple new rounded out a crew of ten, all great people on and off the water. The weather promised sunshine and warm nights, the river level mellow, perfect for a relaxing two-day trip. A couple shuttle drivers helped with logistics and saved us a long drive at the end.

We gathered at the trailhead to pack gear and prepare for the two-mile hike in. This time I rigged a slick backpack system using a pair of webbing straps and an old hip belt to save my shoulder from the heavy lifting—tricks learned over my years in the sport. I strolled leisurely down the trail in no rush to get to the bottom. The hike, the weight, the heat of the sun, all were a grand part of the experience, and I savored every drop of sweat and sharp stone underfoot. What better way to start a new phase of life than the culmination of the previous one, the ultimate kayak trip.

We ate lunch in the shade at the river's edge, waiting for two guys who decided to try a shortcut and got lost in the woods. The delay meant nothing—we had two days, all the time in the world. They showed up chagrined but no one complained as we suited up and hit the water. Barely a ripple of a rapid started the run, but I splashed water in my face as I would before a big drop, letting the cold focus my mind and sharpen my senses. I wanted to take in everything on this trip.

The group moved fluidly with no formal structure and minimal discussions, those more familiar with the run leading those less sure of the route, swapping positions and roles on each rapid and mixing randomly in the flats to carry on conversations with someone new. As alert as I was, none of the rapids stuck in my memory. What lasted was the image of Matt holding his arms to the heavens rejoicing against a backdrop of a giant granite slab, the sound of Alex laughing as we boofed the same rock at the same time to land on top of each other, the smile on Liz's face as she recounted her first time down the river. Sure, we had one swim at Upper Freeman, the rapid where I first swam on my ill-fated attempt on the Forks my first season of boating. That's part of the sport and no one's mood had dampened when we stopped at a flat shelf beneath pine trees to camp for the night.

The evening created as many memories as the paddling. The granite spires high above us glowing in the sunset, Matt stomping on logs to create firewood, the flask of fine whiskey circling the group as we swapped tales around a flickering fire. More than one person asked if I planned to undertake another paddling odyssey now that I had no job.

"No," I replied. "I plan to write."

A few nods and smiles showed their simple support, much as when I decided to run Royal Flush. Maybe it was risky, the chances for success small and disaster high. But my friends supported my decision and stood ready to help if needed. That was more than enough for me.

We woke with the sun but took our time over breakfast and breaking camp, no one eager for the day's conclusion. The bigger rapids lay below us, still packing enough punch to make folks nervous. I portaged Vortex with Gilbert, not out of fear but solidarity. I ran Carson's Falls for much the same reason, taking more pleasure from others' ugly but successful runs than my own graceful line. No one had anything to prove but everyone took their shot, nothing but smiles on the downstream side regardless of the result. I finished up as happy and excited as the first time I completed the Forks without swimming. Matt and I drove back through the Sierra, scouting potential creeks and marveling at the beauty in the world.

This was my place in the paddling world. I no longer needed to push myself, no longer needed to improve or find new challenges. Perfection wasn't to be found in the paddling but in the experience. I could paddle or not, charge hard or cruise easy, simply enjoy whatever I did with no outside forces driving my goals. I could be happy in the moment—and before and after.

I didn't kayak much for the next several months, but paddling was a big part of my life. I started my novel, facing challenges and doubts along the way. But I put my head down and kept going forward. When I finished, it wasn't perfect, so I studied and practiced and tried again. My father passed away after months in the hospital. I leaned on friends for support and let them carry the load for a while. I left safe water behind and put myself out into the world where I met my future wife. Together we moved to the Mendocino coast to build a life together, full of joy and adventure. I returned to the sea with a new partner and to the rivers and polo pitch with old friends.

I am very much a kayaker these days and always will be, no matter how long between paddles or how much my skills deteriorate. Kayaking is a part of who I am. It's the part that carries boats for those who can't lift them and waits at the top of a rapid to guide down the less experienced. It's the drive to be the best and test yourself against forces you cannot overcome but only hope to ride. It shares sorrows and joys with friends and strangers, the only requirements to join are a desire to try and the willingness to fail. In many ways kayaking is the best part of me, and I hope I give it my best in return.

Bryant Burkhardt grew up in a small farm town in Minnesota. He moved to California for graduate school in physics and stumbled into a career in middle management. After being introduced to kayaking on the Pacific Ocean, it didn't take long to realize passion should lead, not follow, and he chased his dream of kayaking for a living. *A Paddler's Journey* follows that trail through kayaking and life. He continues to teach and blog about the sport at *www.paddleca.com* though his passion for writing has broadened into fiction under his pen name of Blair B. Burke.

22285321R00113

Printed in Poland
by Amazon Fulfillment
Poland Sp. z o.o., Wrocław